The Middle Ages

1000 Interesting Facts About the Medieval Period

Welcome Aboard, Check Out This Limited-Time Free Bonus!

Ahoy, reader! Welcome to the Ahoy Publications family, and thanks for snagging a copy of this book! Since you've chosen to join us on this journey, we'd like to offer you something special.

Check out the link below for a FREE e-book filled with delightful facts about American History.

But that's not all - you'll also have access to our exclusive email list with even more free e-books and insider knowledge. Well, what are ye waiting for? Click the link below to join and set sail toward exciting adventures in American History.

Access your bonus here: https://ahoypublications.com/

Or, Scan the QR code!

Table of Contents

Introduction

Dive into the alluring yet tumultuous world of medieval times, a period that shaped our modern-day society. From **the rise of Christianity to Charlemagne's reign and Viking expansion to the Crusades,** discover how these pivotal moments forever altered human history. Unearth various **intriguing facts about Muslim expansion, the papacy, monarchies, and the increase in education.** Relive remarkable battles during **the Reconquista** and **Mongol invasions, and explore Gothic literature and architecture.**

Embark on an adventure to **uncover fascinating stories and explore the medieval period!**

Rise of Christianity
(4th–7th centuries)

Christianity rose from a persecuted cult to become one of the world's major religions. This chapter will explore facts about **this remarkable transformation,** including its spread across Europe and Asia Minor, **the role of Emperor Constantine** in unifying Christian beliefs, and the emergence of monasticism.

1. **Christianity started as a small movement and emerged from Judaism in the 1st century CE.**

2. **Roman authorities initially persecuted the religion,** but it grew rapidly and officially became recognized as a religion in Rome in 313 with the Edict of Milan.

3. By late antiquity, **Christianity was the most popular religion in western Europe,** Asia Minor, and North Africa before the rise of Islam in the 7th century.

4. **Books such as the Bible,** On the Incarnation by Athanasius, and **The City of God by Saint Augustine** helped spread the Christian faith during this period. **These works provided moral guidance and philosophical answers** that appealed to many people in turbulent times.

5. In 325, **Emperor Constantine called the first ecumenical council—the Council of Nicaea—to unify Christian beliefs.** This meeting marked a significant milestone in Christianity's growth and influence.

6. **The Nicene Creed** (325) affirmed **Christians' belief in one God in three persons:** the **Father, Son, and Holy Spirit, establishing Trinitarianism** as a central tenet of orthodox Christianity.

7. In 380, **Emperor Theodosius declared Nicene Christianity to be Rome's official faith,** suppressing other religions, including paganism and heretical **Christian sects like Arianism** (the belief that Jesus was not of the same substance as God).

8. **The First Council of Constantinople,** held one year later, also affirmed **the Nicene Creed; this strengthened the Trinitarian belief,** though the council only hosted Eastern bishops, to the disappointment of **the Church of Rome.**

9. In 391, **Theodosius banned all forms of pagan worship and ordered that Christian practices** be observed throughout the Roman Empire.

10. **The Justinian Code** (529–565), written **by Emperor Justinian,** listed laws **governing the Roman Empire,** including those concerning religious practices.

11. **With Roman support and protection, Christianity spread rapidly across Europe and beyond in the 4th century.**

12. In 410, **Rome was sacked by the Visigoths, weakening Rome's political power over territories,** which opened up opportunities for missionary work from Christians who sought to bring their faith into new lands.

13. **Monasticism was an important part of early Christianity. Saint Anthony** is credited with establishing the first monastery in Egypt between 300 and 310.

14. **The Benedictine Order emerged around 530 and had rules like working,** living communally, praying, and providing hospitality to those who needed it.

15. **Saint Jerome translated the Bible into Latin between 383 and 404,** which became the authoritative text used by the Roman Church.

16. **Saint Augustine was one of the most successful Christian missionaries,** helping spread Christianity throughout North Africa.

17. In fact, **Saint Augustine's writings would become even more influential during the Late Middle Ages,** leading to the creation of the Order of Saint Augustine, which was based in the Italian region of Tuscany and was created in the 13th century.

18. In 451, **the Council of Chalcedon was held to confirm Christian beliefs and practices,** particularly concerning the dual nature of **Jesus Christ** as both divine and human.

19. **The 5th century saw the rise of new heresies, such as monophysitism and Nestorianism,** which threatened unity amongst believers.

20. By 600, **Christianity had become a significant faith with millions of adherents across Europe,** Asia Minor, and North Africa. It was especially popular among the former Roman aristocracy and their descendants.

21. **Pope Gregory I (590–604) is credited with launching the Gregorian mission.** He sent monks to Ireland, Scotland, and England, where they converted pagans from the Celtic faiths/ Druidism to Christianity.

22. In 664, **the Synod of Whitby dealt with different church practices in England and reaffirmed the status of Christianity.** This marked a significant turning point for English Christianity, as English missionaries began traveling worldwide to spread Christianity.

23. **Saint Boniface, the most well-known English missionary, traveled across Germany,** spreading the gospel during the 8th century.

24. **Monasticism flourished in Ireland during the medieval period, with many saints, including Saint Patrick, preaching Christianity to the local population.** Monasteries in Ireland were established as early as the 5th century.

25. **Irish missionaries took Christianity to Scotland and Northumbria in the 6th century.** Their impact was so great that many pagan tribes converted quickly.

26. By the 8th century, **Christianity was the dominant faith in Anglo-Saxon England**

27. Differences in **the Christian** religion would spark tensions between the East and West. The Christian faith would be split into two main religions with **the Great Schism** in 1054.

28. In 610, **Islam was founded and began its spread across the Middle East and North Africa.** The spread of this religion posed a challenge to Christian authorities since they had previously enjoyed a near-monopoly on faith in these regions.

29. **The Islamic conquest of Jerusalem in 638 marked a significant turning point for both faiths.** The Catholic Church maintained control over parts of the city and important holy sites like the Church of **the Holy Sepulchre,** but it became increasingly challenging to protect pilgrimage routes from Muslim attacks.

30. **The spread of Islam caused political tensions between Muslims and Christians.** The Islamic conquest eventually reached Iberia.

Fall of the Western Roman Empire
(476)

The fall of the Western Roman Empire marked a pivotal moment in European history. After centuries of cultural and political dominance, **Rome was overthrown by the Germanic tribes.** Learn how the fall of Rome impacted Rome with these interesting facts.

31. **The Western Roman Empire officially ended in 476 when the last Western emperor, Romulus Augustus, was deposed by Odoacer.**

32. **Rome had been under continual attack since the 4th century** and faced a series of **barbarian invasions** from **Germanic tribes**, such as **the Visigoths, Ostrogoths, and Vandals.**

33. **Although many people blame the barbarians for the collapse of the Roman Empire,** we have to acknowledge that Rome had been on the decline for centuries. The barbarian invasions only helped accelerate the process of its demise.

34. **Some believe the decline of the Roman Empire began after Emperor Constantine moved his court eastward to Byzantium.** He established Constantinople as the new capital city of the empire in 330.

35. In 395, **Roman Emperor Theodosius I divided the empire in half, with his sons Honorius ruling over the Western Roman Empire and Arcadius ruling over the Eastern Roman Empire.**

36. **One of the leading causes behind the Romans losing control over Italy was that they allowed various barbarians to settle in the country.** They eventually became powerful enough to overthrow Rome.

37. In the late 4th century, **there were multiple rebellions in remote Roman provinces,** resulting in losing control in places like Britannia in 410.

38. In 410, **Alaric and his Visigoths sacked Rome for three days,** causing significant destruction, including burning churches and looting homes.

39. In 455, **the Vandals brutally sacked Rome, weakening its position and leading to its eventual fall.**

40. **Military campaigns against Germanic tribes** like **the Visigoths** were largely unsuccessful, making Rome's authority increasingly challenged by these groups.

41. **Rome was further weakened after a disastrous defeat at the Battle of Adrianople,** where Emperor Valens was killed along with two-thirds of the Roman army.

42. **There were also internal conflicts between different factions within the Roman Senate that exacerbated the instability,** further weakening Rome's power base.

43. **Christianity began to take hold across Europe during this time.** As a result, many people were more loyal to the church than to Rome, leading to the fragmentation of loyalties.

44. **Some scholars believe the peaceful nature of Christianity made Romans reluctant to fight in wars,** leading to a decrease in manpower.

45. **The Roman currency became increasingly devalued due to the constant wars,** weakening economic stability and reducing tax revenues.

46. **After the Western Roman Empire fell, there was no single ruler over Europe. Instead,** there were separate kingdoms formed by Germanic tribes or warlords.

47. **The fall of the Western Roman Empire marks the beginning of the Middle Ages,** which lasted until the Renaissance around the 14th century when European society once again began embracing classical knowledge from ancient Greece and Rome.

48. **Although the Western Roman Empire officially ended in 476,** the Eastern Roman or Byzantine Empire continued until 1453, when Constantinople finally fell to the Ottoman Turks.

49. **The fall of the Western Roman Empire also roughly marks the beginning of the rise of the feudal system, where people were bound to their lord through the land.** Workers were granted some rights but also had many obligations, such as providing military service.

50. **Due to the instability in Europe, a period of stagnation began,** with the continent falling behind in technological innovations to the Middle East and China.

51. **The Latin language underwent significant changes and eventually evolved into the Romance languages spoken in most European countries today,** especially those in the Mediterranean region.

52. **Roman law continued to exist in some form even after the Western Roman Empire ended,** with the Justinian Code being one of the most influential legal documents from this period still used today.

53. **Roman art and architecture experienced significant changes during the empire's fall,** most notably with the introduction of Christian-style churches, which replaced pagan temples.

54. **Migration patterns changed drastically.** Many people moved away from cities into rural areas, seeking safety against invasions or for more land to farm.

55. **With Rome's fall, trade routes became disrupted,** leading Europe's economy into a recession that lasted centuries before it was able to recover with the establishment of new trading networks.

56. **Although the Germanic tribes caused much destruction,** they also contributed significantly to European culture by introducing different customs, such as language, clothing styles, and music.

57. **This period saw the emergence of nation-states like France, Spain, and Britain,** which developed from the previous tribal structures that had been in place.

58. **Some barbarian warlords embraced Christianity to legitimize themselves as successors to the Roman emperor,** while others continued to practice their own religions.

59. **The fall of the Western Roman Empire remains one of the most compelling subjects to study,** as it is very complex and is often used as a reference when other empires fail.

60. **The reasons behind the Western Roman Empire's fall are widespread and systematic political and socio-cultural effects,** the likes of which had never been felt throughout Europe before.

The Byzantine Empire
(4th–15th centuries)

Explore the enthralling history of the Byzantine Empire, which lasted for over one thousand years and, at its height, controlled much of **the Balkans, Anatolia, the Levant, and Egypt.**

61. **The Byzantine Empire, also known as the Eastern Roman Empire,** was established in the 4th century CE and lasted for about a thousand years, ceasing to exist in 1453.

62. **The name "Byzantine" comes from Byzantium,** which was the original name of the settlement upon which **Constantinople was built.**

63. **Roman Emperor Constantine the Great reorganized the Roman Empire in 330,** splitting it into two separate territories to make it easier to govern.

64. **The Eastern Roman Empire, with its capital Constantinople,** slowly diverged from the Western Roman Empire due to its distinct **Hellenistic culture** in comparison to **the Latin culture of the West**.

65. **The Byzantine Empire survived the fall of Rome in 476,** continuing to exist as a separate entity until its eventual collapse.

66. **The Byzantine emperor would consider himself the de facto new leader of the former lands of the Western Roman Empire,** though this never actually materialized into political power in that region.

67. **The Byzantines even referred to themselves as Romans, preserving the cultural and legal legacy of the ancient Roman Empire** when its Western counterpart fell.

68. **While the rest of Europe was warring with each other, the Byzantine scholars preserved and studied ancient Greek and Roman texts,** contributing to the revival of classical learning during the Renaissance.

69. **The empire's bureaucracy was highly organized,** with civil servants divided into several classes based on their duties and responsibilities.

70. **The Byzantine legal system incorporated Roman law and later Christian principles,** contributing to the development of civil and religious laws.

71. **The empire would reach its greatest extent during the reign of Justinian I** (r. 527–565), who is remembered as one of the most successful rulers in Roman history.

72. **Justinian launched military campaigns to reconquer much of the lost territories in the West,** reclaiming parts of the western Mediterranean, the North African coast, and Italy.

73. **In addition to successful military conquests,** Justinian is remembered for his contributions to the establishment of a new civil code.

74. **His reign also marked the time when Christianity cemented itself as the most widespread religion in the Byzantine Empire.**

75. **Christianity became the official religion of the empire during the reign of Theodosius I in the 4th century,** but it took a long time for it to become a mainstream religion practiced by the majority.

76. **After Justinian's death, the reconquered territories came under direct threat from barbarians,** making it impossible for its successors to hold them, beginning a long period of slow decline for the Byzantine Empire.

77. **In the 7th century, with the rise of Islam, the Byzantine Empire lost control of virtually all of its lands in the Middle East,** as the Muslim caliphates defeated the Byzantine forces repeatedly.

78. **The Battle of Yarmouk in 636 marked the first major defeat of the Byzantines by the Islamic forces,** leading to the loss of the Levant.

79. **In fact, between 674 and 678, the Arabs would even lay siege to Constantinople itself,** though the Byzantines would emerge victorious, organizing a defense under Emperor Constantine IV.

80. **In this battle, the Byzantines used a powerful weapon called Greek fire,** which was a highly flammable substance that was very effective against wooden ships.

81. **The Arabs laid siege to Constantinople again between 717 and 718 but were unsuccessful,** as the Byzantines utilized trebuchets to launch disease-ridden corpses and animals over the city walls to weaken the Arab besiegers.

82. As time went on, **the differences between the Byzantine Empire and the rest of the Christian world** slowly started to become more apparent when it came to understanding Christian dogma and ceremonial practices.

83. **In the 8th and 9th centuries, the empire would be dominated by a religious controversy over the matter of icons,** which would eventually lead to iconoclasm emerging as a distinct feature of Eastern Christianity.

84. **When the Christian Church officially split into two in the 11th century,** the Byzantine Empire was already very much alienated, both culturally and politically, from the West, making it even more difficult to withstand new invasions.

85. **During this period, the empire was threatened not only from the east but also from the northwest,** as the migrating Bulgar and Khazar peoples forced the emperor to make concessions in the Balkans.

86. In 867, **Basil I became the emperor, establishing the Macedonian dynasty,** which marked a brief period of revival of the Byzantine Empire for about 150 years.

87. **The Byzantine Empire started to strike back against the Muslims in the east,** sometimes with the help of the newly Christianized Slavic peoples of eastern Europe.

88. In 1071, **the Byzantines suffered a devastating defeat against the Seljuks at the Battle of Manzikert in Anatolia.** The Byzantines had to give up much of eastern Anatolia to the new conquerors.

89. **This defeat served as one of the reasons behind the launching of the Crusades, a**s Constantinople begged the West for help against Muslim invaders.

90. **Despite the relative success of the early Crusaders,** the Byzantine Empire would never recover from the Seljuk invasion. It continued its decline for the next three centuries.

91. In 1204, **the empire would almost completely collapse after the capture of Constantinople during the Fourth Crusade,** leading to the fragmentation of former Byzantine territories in the Balkans and Anatolia and the establishment of the Latin Empire.

92. **These new states would challenge each other for dominance in the region,** but neither would be strong enough to contest the new rising **Muslim power** in the form of **the Ottoman Turks.**

93. Continuous conflicts with the Ottomans weakened what was left of the Byzantine Empire, with **the Battle of Ankara in 1402 resulting in the Ottoman capture of Emperor Manuel II Palaiologos.**

94. **The final Ottoman siege of Constantinople in 1453, under Mehmed II** (also known as **Mehmed the Conqueror**), led to the fall of the city and **the end of the Byzantine Empire.**

95. **The fall of Constantinople marked the end of the Roman Empire's millennia-long existence** and marked the transition to **the Ottoman Empire's dominance in the region.**

Barbarian Invasions and Migration
(5th–8th centuries)

Between the 5th and 8th centuries, Germanic tribes like the Visigoths, Ostrogoths, Vandals, and Lombards invaded Roman provinces. This period saw a **shift from Roman emperors toward Germanic-speaking rulers,** allowing new kingdoms to emerge. Let's look at how **the barbarian tribes** impacted the makeup of Europe during **the Middle Ages.**

96. **The fall of the Western Roman Empire** can be contextualized into a larger framework of **barbarian invasions and migration waves in Europe** and the Near East, which lasted from the 5th to the 8th century.

97. **The word "barbarian" originates from ancient Greece.** It was used by the Greeks to refer to people who were alien, inferior, and uncivilized in their eyes.

98. **Ancient Romans adopted the word to refer to the different non-Romans** they conquered throughout the centuries.

99. **During these invasions, much of western Europe came to be populated by Germanic people groups** who had left their homelands in search of new land or because of political turmoil.

100. **The Roman Empire** tried to keep **the barbarians** at bay for centuries.

101. **The Romans closely monitored their borders** and waged constant wars to keep the barbarians out.

102. **However, the empire was forced to open its borders and let the barbarians settle in Roman lands in the 4th century** due to the many migrants knocking at its door.

103. **The barbarians were victorious against the Romans at times, such as in the Battle of the Teutoburg Forest in 9 CE,** when an alliance of barbarian tribes in Germany defeated Roman legions.

104. **Barbarian fighters were known for their ferocity and zeal but were usually no match for the Romans unless they fought on their own terms.**

105. Interestingly, the Eastern Roman Empire was relatively unaffected by barbarian invasions, managing to hold out and not let them cause instability on the same level as in the West.

106. The Eastern Roman Empire was certainly affected by migratory waves and conflicts, but the East had more professional armies and a more stable government and economy.

107. People from other parts of Eurasia moved into the empire, with the Avars settling around Hungary and the Bulgars entering Thrace.

108. The Picts migrated from Scotland into northern England; the Celts moved southward into France; the Angles, Saxons, and Jutes settled in Britain; and the Franks advanced eastward across Germany.

109. These migrations allowed different cultures to mix with each other, creating new customs and ideas about how to rule and live.

110. Latin became less spoken, and Christianity began to spread rapidly in Europe.

111. People from different parts of Eurasia could communicate with each other without having to learn Latin first. This made emerging new languages, such as the Germanic tongue, and Romance languages, like French, Spanish, and Italian, more accessible.

112. The migrations caused other changes in Europe, such as the introduction of heavily armored cavalry units. These new military techniques would be used for centuries to come.

113. Slavic people migrating eastward from their homeland near modern-day Poland created a new group of languages known as Slavic languages.

114. Arabic speakers coming to Spain gave rise to Moorish Spanish.

115. One of the most influential barbarian leaders was Odoacer, who deposed Romulus Augustus—the last emperor of the Western Roman Empire—in 476, which marked the end of classical antiquity and began medieval times.

116. Back then, many people believed the barbarian invasions were an act of divine punishment; for example, the Huns, led by Attila, were seen as the scourge of God when they invaded and decimated much of eastern Europe in the 5th century.

117. Migrating westward from central Asia, the Hunnic hordes defeated everyone on their way and caused great havoc to the Romans.

118. The Huns were expert horse riders and experienced mounted warriors. Their use of mounted warfare allowed them to defeat almost everyone they encountered.

119. Many barbarians adopted Christianity during this period.

120. Barbarian tribes were sometimes influenced by Roman missionaries or converted through contact with other Christians living nearby, like the Franks.

121. These invasions were responsible for ushering in medieval Europe, which would become one of the most influential periods in history with its unique style of architecture, art, and literature.

122. Barbarian leaders would eventually create kingdoms in different regions out of the remnants of the Western Roman Empire.

123. The Visigoths took over Iberia and southern France.

124. The Vandals established themselves in North Africa.

125. The Saxons, Franks, Jutes, Burgundians, Alamanni, and Suebi took over significant parts of the former **Western Roman Empire,** but their state-like formations were initially small, unlike those of **the Visigoths or the Vandals.**

Anglo-Saxon England
(5th-11th centuries)

The Anglo-Saxons are well known in history for taking over Britain. Discover thirty interesting facts about how they settled the island and gained power.

126. **The island of Great Britain was under the control of the Roman Empire for over three centuries,** from the mid-1st century CE to the collapse of the Western Roman Empire in 476 CE.

127. **At the beginning of the 5th century, as the Roman Empire struggled to keep up with the barbarian migration in its lands,** Emperor Constantine III made a decision to withdraw the Roman forces from Britannia to support other contingents in mainland Europe.

128. **For the rulers of the province,** this meant they had to essentially look after themselves.

129. **To defend themselves from the raids of the Picts in modern-day Scotland,** they decided to increasingly recruit Germanic tribes as mercenaries in their armies. **This followed a larger trend in the**

later stages of the Western Roman Empire, where Romans employed foreign tribesmen, a practice that proved to be unsustainable in the long run.

130. **Most of the warriors the Roman officials in Britannia recruited were Angles and Saxons,** who had mostly dwelt in the areas of modern-day northern Germany and Denmark.

131. **Eventually, it is believed the Anglo-Saxons migrated to Britain in large masses,** settling in coastal towns and slowly taking over the heartland of the island.

132. **The Anglo-Saxons pushed the local Briton population,** which had lived on the island even before the Roman conquest, more toward the west.

133. **The Romano-Britons resisted the mass migration and even defeated the Anglo-Saxons around 500 at the Battle of Mount Badon,** an occurrence that is believed to have temporarily stopped the Anglo-Saxon takeover of Britain for a time.

134. However, by around 600, the Angles had almost fully taken over the central and eastern parts of the island. The Saxons controlled much of the south, while the local Briton population was forced to the modern-day nation of Wales.

135. The Anglo-Saxons developed their own state-like formations. There were seven different political entities in total, and they would come to be known as **the Heptarchy** (from the Greek word hepta, meaning seven).

136. There were four major and three minor Anglo-Saxon kingdoms in the Heptarchy: Mercia, Wessex, Northumbria, and East Anglia were the major kingdoms, and Essex, Kent, and Sussex were the minor kingdoms.

137. The kingdoms of the Heptarchy would challenge each other for dominance in the region for several centuries.

138. The Anglo-Saxons eventually adopted Christianity. Saint Patrick is credited with helping to convert the Anglo-Saxons and Picts, although his main claim to fame is bringing Christianity to much of Ireland.

139. It is believed the first Anglo-Saxon to have converted to Christianity was King Ethelbert of Kent (c. 560–616), who would emerge as one of the most interesting figures of early medieval England.

140. Ethelbert married Bertha, the daughter of Charibert I, the king of Franks, forging a short-lasting but powerful alliance that led to **the Kingdom of Kent's** brief dominance in **the Heptarchy.**

141. Ethelbert is also credited with the creation of the earliest written Germanic legal codex, Ethelbert's Law.

142. In the 8th century, **the Heptarchy was confronted with the biggest threat it had faced yet: the raiding Vikings from Scandinavia.**

143. **Britain was perhaps the most favored destination of the Vikings.** After reaching British shores in the late 8th century, at Lindisfarne, the Vikings would return with a huge force in 865 with the aim of conquering the English kingdoms.

144. **This Viking force was described by the English as the Great Heathen Army.** The Viking army was able, with reinforcements over the years, to take over almost all of the northern and central English territories.

145. **The Kingdom of Northumbria, which took the brunt of the initial Viking assault,** fell first in 867, then came East Anglia in 869, and then most of Mercia in 877.

146. **Only the Kingdom of Wessex was able to withstand the Viking invasions.** The kingdom was even able to defeat **the Vikings at the Battle of Edington** in 878, led by their king, Alfred the Great.

147. **Alfred the Great is remembered as one of the most powerful kings during the Heptarchy.** In addition to defending his kingdom from the Vikings, he was a great ruler who introduced administrative and military reforms, built a system of defenses throughout England, and supported the arts and culture.

148. **In his later years, Alfred began the unification process of England by trying to take over the Anglo-Saxon territories** that had survived the Viking raids.

149. **Alfred's successors went on the offensive and took back control of East Anglia in the first decade of the 10th century.**

150. **King Athelstan annexed Northumbria in 927** and defeated a large army of enemy **Danes and Scots at the Battle of Brunanburh** in 937, emerging as the first king of a united England.

151. However, **despite Athelstan's victories, it would take his successors a lot of effort to keep hold of the conquered territories,** especially in the north and especially as Viking raids resumed on a larger scale in the late 10th century.

152. **The throne of England was eventually claimed by Cnut, the son of King Sweyn of Denmark,** after a succession struggle that saw **Edmund II** die under suspicious circumstances.

153. **Although a foreigner took the throne in 1016,** the end of Anglo-Saxon rule is thought to have ended when William the Conqueror took power in 1066.

154. **The history of Anglo-Saxon England is relatively well documented in the Anglo-Saxon Chronicle**—a collection of annals that was most likely compiled around the late 9th century under **Alfred the Great** and was even updated in the following centuries.

155. **This period provides crucial insights into many of the cultural and political aspects of post-Anglo-Saxon Britain,** like the administrative or linguistic divisions that still exist to this day.

Muslim Expansion
(7th–15th centuries)

This chapter will explore the fascinating history of Muslim expansion between the 7th and 15th centuries. We'll explore the Islamic Golden Age and discover how the Muslims were able to expand their domain so quickly.

156. **The Muslim expansion began in the 7th century** with **the rise of Islam** and saw Muslims conquering much of southwest Asia, North Africa, and parts of Europe by the 8th century.

157. **This period is often referred to as the Islamic Golden Age when science, technology, and art flourished under Muslim rule,** first between 750 and 1200 CE and later on during the heyday of the Ottoman Empire up to the end of the 16th century.

158. **The Islamic Golden Age saw marvelous advances in the fields of science, mathematics, and medicine,** but these discoveries would not reach the Christian world until centuries later when contact with the Arabic world became more established.

159. **Inventions like the astrolabe were created in Muslim countries and had a major impact on life,** which led to the educated minorities of Muslim states becoming more sophisticated compared to their European counterparts.

160. **Muslim rulers collaborated with Arab physicians and scientists to make advances in medicine.** These advances were based on the works of Greek doctors, such as Hippocrates and Galen.

161. **During this era, some major cities, like Córdoba (Spain),** were founded or greatly expanded due to their strategic location as crossroads for trade routes or good defensive sites.

162. **One outcome of the Muslim expansion was the Arabization—the spread of Arabic culture, language, and customs—of places like North Africa and the Levant,** where populations were not traditionally Arab.

163. **Military conquest was not the only way Islam spread.** Islamic culture and education were disseminated through **universities, such as Al-Azhar in Cairo,** which still stands today as one of the oldest active universities for higher learning.

164. **Taxation was an important factor in the expansion of provinces.** Taxes were collected from different areas and used to fund public projects, such as mosques, schools, and other infrastructure. This allowed for growth without requiring much labor or resources from local populations.

165. **The spread of Sufism helped the Muslim expansion.** This doctrine guided people who wanted answers outside traditional religious teachings.

166. **Sufism allowed people access to inner peace while still following Islamic laws and principles from the Quran.** People also benefited from the social acceptance that came with it. To this day, Sufism is a major part of Islamic culture.

167. **During this period, Muslims established trade centers along the Silk Road, which connected eastern Asia to Europe.** The Silk Road led to great economic prosperity due to the influx of goods, services, and ideas between different regions.

168. In the 8th century, **Caliph al-Mansur ordered the construction of Baghdad,** which served as the capital city for the Abbasid dynasty and became a hub of learning during its golden age under Islamic rule.

169. **Muslim rulers built grand monuments like the Great Mosque of Damascus and sites in Mecca and Medina to honor their religion** and display respect and power.

170. **From the 8th to the 10th century, paper mills were established in different parts of the Muslim world, like Egypt and Syria.** This allowed people to write down knowledge and other information easily. As a result, literacy spread among those living under Islamic rule.

171. **A banking system was developed in the Islamic world,** which made trading easier than before and provided security against theft.

172. **Regional Islamic schools mostly taught children about religion and its associated values.** Schools also taught reading and writing, which led to a significant increase in education levels over the centuries.

173. **The Muslim expansion saw the rise of powerful empires like the Umayyad,** which would go on to conquer much of Iberia and southern France before being defeated by the Franks at the Battle of Tours (732).

174. **The Fatimid and Ayyubid dynasties would emerge in North Africa,** challenging the Crusaders and the newly arrived Turkic peoples from central Asia.

175. **The Umayyad Caliphate was the second caliphate that was established after the death of Prophet Muhammad.** It expanded into Arabia, Persia, North Africa, Iberia, and Anatolia.

176. **The Umayyad Caliphate would be succeeded by the Abbasid Caliphate in 750,** which would further spread Islam into former Persian lands and parts of central Asia.

177. From the 8th century onward, **many places that had been taken over by the Muslims were Arabicized, with Islam emerging as a dominant religion.** Muslim rulers put more pressure on Christian states, especially the Byzantine Empire.

178. **The Arab caliphates would eventually start to grow weaker after pressure from the Crusaders and the Turkic peoples,** who migrated and conquered much of the Muslim world.

179. **The Seljuks would take over much of the Middle East by the late 11th century.** Since they adopted Islam themselves, they started a new era of Muslim expansion.

180. **After the conquest of the Turks, Muslim realms would be significantly expanded after the rise of the Ottoman Empire,** which would have its heyday in the 15th and 16th centuries. Before that time, many Islamic states often fought each other for the same territories.

The Reconquista
(711–1492)

For centuries, the Iberian Peninsula was embroiled in a long and complex struggle for control between Muslim forces and the Christian kingdoms of Castile, Aragon, Navarre, Portugal, and other European states. This conflict is known as the Reconquista, which ultimately led to the expulsion of Muslims from Spain or their conversion to Christianity. We'll explore how this bloody war shaped Spanish society and impacted Europe.

181. **The Reconquista was a centuries-long struggle to reclaim the Iberian Peninsula from Muslim rule.**

182. It began in 711 **when Muslims conquered much of Visigothic Hispania** and continued until 1492 with **the fall of Granada**, which marked the end of Islamic rule in the peninsula.

183. Different **Muslim states controlled Iberia and the North African coast during this period,** most notably **the Caliphate of Córdoba** (929–1031) and **the Almohad dynasty** (1121–1269).

184. Despite the fact that these Muslim states were independent and succeeding political entities, **the Christians nevertheless referred to them as the Moors,** a term that was used to describe Muslim or Arab populations in Iberia, North Africa, and Sicily.

185. **The Reconquista was a conscious effort to take back the territories the Christians** had lost to Islamic forces in the 7th and 8th centuries.

186. **The Reconquista also saw an internal struggle among different Christian kingdoms,** such as Castile, Aragon, Navarre, and Portugal.

187. **Pope Gregory VII encouraged Spanish Christians to take up arms against Muslims during the 11th century,** resulting in increased holy wars ("crusades") that further contributed to the Muslims' defeat.

188. In 1135, **Alfonso VI declared himself emperor of Spain after reconquering Toledo from Moorish forces,** though a unified Spain would emerge only a couple of centuries later.

189. **The most important figure associated with the Christian victory over Muslim forces is King Ferdinand III, who captured Córdoba,** Seville, and other cities between 1217 and 1252, bringing about a significant turning point in the war.

190. **Ferdinand III also secured a permanent union between the two Iberian crowns of Castile and León,** which made it easier to fight the Muslims.

191. **Internal divisions and rivalries often hindered Muslim forces,** which led to a decline in their power in Iberia.

192. By 1250, **most of Iberia was under Christian control except for a portion known as the Emirate of Granada,** which held out until 1492.

193. In 1475, **King Ferdinand II of Aragon married Queen Isabella I of Castile,** an event that basically unified two of the largest Catholic crowns in Iberia and served as a basis for a united Spanish kingdom.

194. **With Spain essentially unified, the Christians were easily able to expel whatever Muslim** forces remained in the southern part of the peninsula.

195. **Granada eventually fell to King Ferdinand and Queen Isabella's forces.** The Spanish rulers also launched successful campaigns against other Moorish strongholds in Africa during this period.

196. **During the Reconquista, the Christian forces were often outnumbered but had superior tactics and technology.** The zeal with which they fought to reclaim what they thought was rightfully theirs played a big role in their eventual success.

197. **During the Crusades, a few military expeditions were organized to help the Christians against the Muslims in Iberia.**

198. **Catholic military orders, most importantly the Knights Templar and the Order of Santiago,** played an important role during the Reconquista.

199. **Catholic rulers would often grant military orders control of strategically important castles,** and the military orders would hold them with their own forces.

200. **The military orders took part in military campaigns. Their members were professional and devout warriors,** which made them excellent fighters on the battlefield.

201. **The end of the Reconquista was followed by the Christians'** effort to homogenize the population of Iberia under one faith.

202. **Muslims and other religious minorities, namely the Jews,** were harshly persecuted and forced to convert to Christianity.

203. **The end of the Reconquista coincided with the rise of the Spanish Inquisition,** one of the most infamous and intolerant institutions toward non-Catholic religious populations.

204. Though many **Muslims fled Iberia after the defeat of the Emirate of Granada** in the late 15th century, those who stayed eventually became a recognized minority by the Spanish Crown.

205. **These Muslims were referred to as the Mudejars and were allowed to practice their religion** and customs in small communities throughout Spain.

206. **The Muslim presence had a lasting influence on Spanish art, language** (with hundreds of words adopted from Arabic), music, literature, architecture, and science.

207. **As Moorish influence waned, new forms of music developed, such as flamenco,** which blended Islamic and European elements.

208. **Islamic rule brought about significant advances in science, mathematics, and astronomy** that spread across Europe during this period, which helped fuel further discoveries during the Renaissance.

209. **It is believed around seven million people died during the Reconquista.**

210. **The end of the Reconquista was a major milestone in European history since it marked the end of Muslim rule in the Iberian Peninsula,** a region under Islamic control since 711.

The Papacy
(7th–14th centuries)

The papacy reached its heyday between the 7th and 14th centuries. These interesting facts will talk about the papacy's power and some of the key figures who made a name for themselves.

211. **The pope is the head of the Catholic Church. Saint Peter,** the first bishop of Rome, is considered to be the first pope, though the office would not have this name until much later.

212. **The exact number of popes throughout history is disputed. Some held the office multiple times,** and some only occupied the position for a few days. However, most historians agree that there have been 266 popes in history.

213. **The early history of the papacy is very complicated. During the first three to four centuries after Christianity was created,** it did not play an important role in the Roman Empire.

214. After 476, **the Church of Rome regarded itself as a symbolic successor to the Western Roman Empire.** The papacy began to grow in importance as a result.

215. **Pope Gregory I** (590–604) is rightfully regarded as one of the most influential popes to have ever lived. His efforts led to the pope emerging as the de facto spiritual leader of unstable western Europe after the fall of **the Western Roman Empire.**

216. During this period, **popes started to gain tremendous authority over religious matters and political issues within Europe.**

217. **The Papal States were established in 756 when King Pippin of the Franks** (also known as Pepin the Short) gave large parts of central Italy to the pope, **including Tuscany, Umbria, Marche, Romagna, and Lazio.** This arrangement lasted until 1870 when Italy annexed them.

218. **An important institution of the papacy is the College of Cardinals,** which is composed of cardinals appointed by the pope. Their role is to advise the pope on important matters regarding the Catholic Church and elect future popes when needed.

219. **After the establishment of the Papal States, the pope's power and influence grew exponentially.** Popes would often get involved in international affairs to support or punish Catholic rulers.

220. **Papal influence reached its peak during the era of the Crusades,** which started when Pope Urban II called for the Christians of Europe to unite and reclaim the Holy Land from Muslims in 1095.

221. **The Papal Inquisition was established in the late 12th – early 13th centuries;** it was an institution with an aim to combat heresy throughout **the Christian realms.**

222. **The inquisitors would charge suspected heretics or non-believers with a multitude of crimes,** like blasphemy, and would put them on trial, resulting in the imprisonment or capital punishment of thousands of individuals.

223. **Pope Boniface VIII (1294–1303) was one of the most controversial popes in history.** His attempts to expand papal power and influence over other European rulers eventually led to a schism within the church and multiple excommunications.

224. **He issued a papal bull in 1302 known as Unam sanctam,** which declared the pope had authority over all earthly rulers, including kings. Many European rulers challenged this claim.

225. The papal bull is a special document issued by the pope and can range from declarations of war to excommunication or other forms of disciplinary action.

226. Between 1309 and 1376, **due to internal conflicts within the Papal States and the complex political climate of the time,** seven successive popes resided in the city of Avignon, modern-day France.

227. During the Avignon Papacy, **the French Crown interfered heavily in papal affairs.**

228. **The Avignon Papacy became known for its extreme corruption.** Many French popes abused their positions for personal gain, including granting favors in exchange for money or political support, while neglecting duties assigned within the church.

229. **Pope Gregory XI (1370–1378) was the last French pope and returned to Rome at the request of the Italian people,** who were fed up with the corruption during the Avignon Papacy.

230. **The Papal Schism lasted from 1378 to 1417** when three popes claimed authority over the Catholic Church.

231. **It was finally resolved after a long period of mediation with the election of Pope Martin V in 1417.**

232. **During this period, the pope introduced many reforms, such as banning simony** (selling church offices) and enacting laws to protect clergy from being mistreated by secular authorities.

233. **Innocent III (1198–1216) was one of the most successful and influential popes.** He significantly increased papal power through successful military campaigns and diplomatic negotiations with European rulers, such as **Holy Roman Emperor Frederick II.**

234. **Eventually, the corrupt practices of the church and its vying for power would be recognized during the Protestant Reformation when Martin Luther** and others aimed to eliminate the harmful practices of the church and introduce reforms.

235. **Although the credibility of the church took a severe hit during the Reformation,** the papacy would challenge the reformers during the Counter-Reformation when it tried to reduce the influence of new Protestant religions.

Charlemagne's Reign
(768–814)

From the rise of Pippin III to the crowning of Charlemagne by Pope Leo III on Christmas Day 800, this chapter will explore how and why **Charlemagne became one of the most powerful rulers in Europe.** We'll delve into fascinating facts about his reign, including how he established a strong central government and an empire stretching from Germany to Spain.

236. **Charlemagne, or Charles the Great, is remembered as one of the greatest rulers ever.** He was the king of the Franks and the founder of the Carolingian Empire.

237. **Charlemagne's father, Pippin III** (or Pepin the Short), was also **the king of the Franks**. He ruled over parts of modern-day France, Belgium, and Germany.

238. **The Kingdom of the Franks was a political entity that emerged after the fall of the Western Roman Empire.** It was ruled by the Merovingian dynasty before Pippin's Carolingian line replaced them.

239. **Charlemagne's victories over the Saxons, which lasted from 772 to 804,** allowed him to expand his empire into modern Germany and conquer Lombardy and Bavaria.

240. In 774, **Charlemagne overthrew Lombard King Desiderius,** which marked the start of his reign as the king of the Lombards.

241. **After conquering most of western Europe by the end of the 8th century,** Charlemagne was crowned the new "Roman" emperor by **Pope Leo III on Christmas Day**, 800, making him a holy figurehead for Christianity in Europe and a symbolic successor of the Romans.

242. **Charlemagne's coronation marked the revival of the title of emperor in Europe after the fall of Rome in 476.** The title would continue to be used by Charlemagne's descendants until 888.

243. **Eventually, the king of Germany, Otto I, would be crowned emperor by the pope,** essentially beginning the Holy Roman Empire, which mostly occupied lands in modern-day Germany.

244. **Charlemagne's coronation established a precedent for all subsequent Roman emperors** to be **crowned by the pope until 1806** when **Napoleon abolished it** following his victory over Prussia and Austria-Hungary at Austerlitz (1805).

245. **After Charlemagne's death, the rulers of the Carolingian Empire** would claim to be the successors of the ancient Roman emperors.

246. **His crowning also symbolically put him on the same level of prestige and power as the Byzantine emperor,** making the two figures each other's rivals.

247. **Charlemagne's coronation as the new Roman emperor was a very clever political rule to reinforce his legitimacy,** resulting in him emerging as an ally to the Roman Church.

248. **Charlemagne was an avid promoter of Christianity and the Catholic Church,** helping to spread it across Europe during his reign by building new churches, convoking councils, and appointing bishops who supported doctrine.

249. **Charlemagne encouraged the populations of conquered lands to convert.** Those who did were rewarded with titles and land grants, furthering the religion's reach into these areas. The number of Christian believers grew exponentially during his reign.

250. **Charlemagne was quite intolerant of those who did not accept conversion.** For example, during the infamous massacre of Verden in 782, thousands of Saxons were ordered to be executed by the emperor because of their refusal to convert.

251. **Charlemagne used capitularies, or laws, to maintain order in his empire.** These laws covered many aspects of life, including religion, the justice system, and military organization.

252. **Later rulers, such as Charles V,** followed Charlemagne's example by creating their legal systems based on the same principles.

253. **Charlemagne established a strong central government and an empire stretching from Saxony in Germany** to parts of present-day Spain. It was the largest political entity in Europe after the fall of the Western Roman Empire.

254. **His court was filled with scholars, poets, musicians, and artists,** enabling him to create a culture that reflected his ideals for Europe at the time—one based on Christian teachings and **Greco-Roman antiquity** (including Latin literature).

255. **Charlemagne is credited with reviving classical antiquity culture in Europe** through his efforts to promote literacy and education. This was known as **the Carolingian Renaissance.**

256. **During his rule, he encouraged education by creating schools and ensuring they were staffed with learned people** capable of teaching children basic Latin and other skills, such as reading and writing.

257. **Interestingly, Charlemagne also established diplomatic relations with Muslim rulers after his conquest of Italy.** The Royal Frankish Annals mention that **Caliph Harun al-Rashid of Baghdad** gifted Charlemagne an Asian elephant and a clock, though it's unclear whether or not this is true.

258. **Since Charlemagne united most of Europe in a time of instability and wars,** he is sometimes referred to as the "Father of Europe" (Pater Europae).

259. **Charlemagne chose the city of Aachen, located in modern-day western Germany,** as his capital.

260. **Charlemagne was a great warrior**. He won several battles against powerful enemies like the **Saxons, the Lombards, the Avars, and the Danes,** which allowed him to expand his empire.

261. Charlemagne's military campaigns in modern-day Spain were crucial in preventing **the Muslim rulers of Iberia from launching attacks on Christian Europe.**

262. **He created a system of taxation that funded military campaigns and expansion efforts.**

263. **Charlemagne's rule saw vast cultural progress through increased infrastructure,** trade, commerce, advances in learning, and intellectual development, all of which laid the foundations for modern European civilizations.

264. **One of the most influential conquerors of all time,** Charlemagne will forever be remembered as the person who almost succeeded in restoring the old borders of the Western Roman Empire.

265. **In 814, Charlemagne died after contracting a lung disease and was buried in Aachen.**

The End of the Carolingian Empire
(9th century)

The Carolingian Empire, founded by Charlemagne in 800, was one of the largest and most powerful empires in medieval Europe, spanning modern-day France, Germany, Italy, and beyond. Its breakup was a major event in **the Middle Ages.** Europe no longer had one major power in control, paving the way for the emergence of monarchies. Let's explore some interesting facts about the dissolution of **the Carolingian Empire.**

266. **After Charlemagne's death, his son, Louis the Pious,** faced difficulties in maintaining his father's empire due to internal power struggles among his sons.

267. **The Treaty of Verdun in 843 divided the Carolingian Empire among Louis the Pious's sons,** resulting in the creation of three separate kingdoms: **West Francia, Middle Francia, and East Francia.**

268. **It marked the definitive end of Carolingian unity** and set the stage for the further disintegration of the empire.

269. **The Treaty of Verdun also began the transition from a somewhat centralized imperial structure** to a fragmented system of feudal kingdoms, shaping the course of European history for centuries to come.

270. Despite the empire's breakup, **Charlemagne's legacy as a unifying figure in European history endured,** influencing subsequent notions of empires and kingship.

271. **West Francia, first ruled by Charles the Bald,** included mostly what is modern-day France. It laid the foundation for the future Kingdom of France.

272. **East Francia, first led by Louis the German,** laid the groundwork **for the Holy Roman Empire, with Otto I eventually ascending to power.**

273. **Middle Francia, or Lothringia, was situated between the western and eastern kingdoms.** It was a short-lived and politically unstable entity that eventually dissolved due to internal strife.

274. **The breakup of the Carolingian Empire was exacerbated by external threats, including Viking raids** and invasions that disrupted trade and governance.

275. **These raids continued even after the empire broke up.** Most notably, there was the invasion of a Viking chieftain named Rollo in the 10th century, who was granted lands in northern France in what is now Normandy.

276. **The division of the Carolingian Empire signaled the waning of Charlemagne's imperial ideals** and marked the transition to a more decentralized political landscape.

277. **The breakup of the empire led to the development of distinct cultural centers,** with cities like Paris, Aachen, and Frankfurt becoming prominent in their respective regions.

278. It also allowed **local nobles to establish their own dynasties** and assert greater control over their territories.

279. **The decentralization resulting from the empire's breakup contributed** to the growth of feudalism, as local lords assumed greater authority over their lands and populations.

280. **The Carolingian Empire's division contributed to the development of different linguistic and cultural identities in different regions,** leading to the emergence of various languages and traditions.

281. **Rulers in the fragmented kingdoms often used dynastic marriages to forge alliances and secure support,** shaping the geopolitics of the post-Carolingian era.

282. **Charles the Fat attempted to reunify the Carolingian Empire briefly in 884,** but his inability to effectively manage its affairs led to his deposition.

283. **In East Francia, the dynasty died out with the death of Louis the Child in 911.** Conrad I from the Duchy of Franconia was selected as the new king.

284. **In West Francia, the Carolingians were replaced by the Capetian dynasty.** Hugh Capet I was crowned the new king of the Franks in 987.

285. **The Carolingian dynasty would persist until 1120, as its successors either slowly died** out or lost control to more powerful aristocracies and ruling families.

286. **The empire's division disrupted established trade routes and economic networks,** affecting the flow of goods and resources across former imperial territories.

287. **The division of the empire also influenced the development of religious centers and institutions,** with different regions promoting their own religious practices and affiliations—something that would be combatted by the Inquisition in the later centuries.

288. **The Carolingian Empire's disintegration had significant implications for the papacy,** as it influenced the dynamics of papal politics and alliances.

289. **The divisions established by the Treaty of Verdun** had a lasting impact on modern European political borders.

290. **The dynastic struggles for control over various territories were often marked by conflicts,** alliances, and shifting loyalties among noble families.

291. **The breakup of the Carolingian Empire played a role in the formation of early national identities,** contributing to the diversity of European cultures.

292. **As a response to the collapse of Charlemagne's empire,** new state formations started to emerge east of the empire's former borders, most notably **in Moravia and Bohemia.**

293. **Some of these regions were not fully converted to Christianity** and faced a **constant threat of Frankish invasion from the west,** making them emerge as natural rivals.

294. **Eventually, with the advent of the Holy Roman Empire,** many of these territories would be integrated either through wars or diplomacy.

295. All in all, **the collapse of the Carolingian Empire was a significant event in early medieval history,** leading to the rise of even more social and political instability that would persist until after the Renaissance.

Medieval Italy
(8th–13th centuries)

The Middle Ages impacted some regions of Europe more significantly than others. Let's take a look at how Italy was affected by the changing times of the medieval era with these thirty intriguing facts.

296. **The old Roman province of Italia underwent perhaps one of the most drastic set of changes after the fall of the Western Roman Empire in 476,** with multiple different kingdoms and empires claiming suzerainty over this once-glorious region.

297. **The Ostrogothic Kingdom, which had been founded by Odoacer, the Germanic leader** who ousted the last Roman emperor, was eventually destroyed by **Byzantine Emperor Justinian. Justinian** restored much of Roman control in the central and southern parts of Italy in the 6th century.

298. **Byzantine control of Italy was short-lived. Another Germanic people, the Lombards,** invaded Italy in the late 6th century and conquered much of the peninsula.

299. **The Lombards ran over much of the countryside and devastated any opposition they met,** establishing their capital in the northern city of Pavia.

300. **During the Lombards' control of Italy, the Church of Rome,** which had previously been subject to the Eastern emperor in Constantinople, started to diverge as its own independent institution.

301. **The Lombards would be defeated by Charlemagne, who established Carolingian control** in northern and central Italy by the late 8th century. **Charlemagne was crowned emperor in the year 800 by Pope Leo III.**

302. **Charlemagne gave much of the central Italian territories to the pope and allowed the local Duchy of Benevento** in the south to act as a buffer between his empire and the remaining Byzantine territories in southern Italy.

303. **With the breakup of the Carolingian Empire,** the Carolingian lands in the northern part of Italy would become part of **the Kingdom of Italy under Louis II in 839.**

304. **For the rest of the 9th century, Italy became a target for the Islamic armies** that invaded the peninsula and Sicily from North Africa.

305. **Southern Italy became a battlefield for a variety of interested parties,** including the Byzantines, the Arabs, and the Normans.

306. **The Normans had initially been recruited as mercenaries but eventually** gained de facto independence from their recruiters in the 10th century.

307. **The Kingdom of Italy was eventually absorbed into what would become the Holy Roman Empire.**

308. **The Holy Roman emperor was also nominally the king of Italy.** However, since he spent most of his time in imperial lands in Germany, the lands that he controlled in Italy slowly became decentralized in the absence of authority.

309. **The power vacuum that was created meant the wealthiest nobles could contest each other for dominance,** leading to the emergence of powerful centers in the northern part of Italy.

310. **The relationship between the Holy Roman emperors, who were, above all, German,** and their Italian dominions grew more and more hostile. This led to succession disputes when the emperor died.

311. **The papacy, which had enjoyed its independence and controlled a sizable chunk of land,** continued to be regarded as a separate sacred institution that was Italian in essence. This counterbalanced the authority of the Holy Roman emperor.

312. **While most of the European states, like England and France,** fully embraced the feudal system, the indirect control of Italy by the Holy Roman Empire meant it had a decentralized political system.

313. **Italy's decentralization resulted in multiple city-states that were ruled either by a single wealthy family or an assembly of the most powerful people in the city.**

314. **Many city-states became subject to oligarchic governance,** with the richest individuals holding all the power and dictating political developments.

315. **Wealthy families would acquire the vast majority of their wealth from commerce,** leading to a gradual replacement of the feudal landowning system in most areas.

316. **Most of the common people in Italy enjoyed the benefits of trade and small business** more than other medieval societies.

317. **The Italian cities, while sometimes nominally under imperial control,** developed their own unique identities and emerged as powerful political units on their own.

318. **Venice is probably the best example of this.** It was ruled by a clan of oligarchs and was nominally a republic. **Venice fielded a large navy and derived most of its power from local and international trade.**

319. **The Republic of Venice and the Republic of Genoa established their own trading colonies in different parts of the Mediterranean and the Black Sea,** even reaching faraway places like **Crimea**. They essentially monopolized the control of trade that flowed into Europe from the East.

320. **The Lombard League,** consisting of the most prosperous northern Italian towns, **defeated Holy Roman Emperor Frederick Barbarossa at Legnano** in 1176.

321. T**his victory was followed by the Peace of Constance,** which granted the city-states official exemption from imperial control and the right to self-govern.

322. **The victory at Legnano gave more power to the Italian city-states,** which would continue their growth and socioeconomic development.

323. **This growth eventually provided the circumstances for the birth of the Renaissance in northern Italy,** a revolutionary cultural, scientific, and social movement that would revolutionize **the High Middle Ages.**

324. **However, the Italian city-states were not safe from war. With the end of imperial control,** several actors would emerge over the centuries who tried to submit the Italians to their rule, most notably the French and the Spanish.

325. **All in all, the history of Italy during the Middle Ages is very complicated,** involving a multitude of culturally diverse actors that all challenged each other for dominance.

Norman Italy
[10th–12th centuries]

We're going to shake things up with the timeline and stick with Italy for a moment. Let's take a look at the Norman conquest of Italy, which began in 999, and how it impacted the region.

326. **The Normans, staying true to their Viking blood, went on long journeys across the known world.** They ended up in Sicily in the 10th century and eventually founded their own state.

327. **If local chronicles are to be believed, the Mediterranean had been raided by the Vikings** in the 9th century, with the raids being led by Björn Ironside and Hastein.

328. **Around the same time, the Vikings established land trade routes with the Byzantine Empire** through the lands in eastern Europe that would eventually become Kievan Rus'.

329. **Southern Europe was just as aware of the strength of Viking warriors** and the potential danger they could pose as northern Europe.

330. **In fact, Viking mercenaries were considered an elite infantry unit in the Byzantine Empire. Referred to as the Varangian Guard,** they served directly under the emperor from the 10th century onward.

331. **In the year 1000, Italy was very decentralized, with the southern part of the peninsula split between the influence of the Byzantines and the remaining Lombards.**

332. **It was in this political climate that the first Normans arrived in southern Italy,** staying with Prince Guaimar of the small Principality of Salerno on their way to Jerusalem in the late 10th century.

333. **At the time of their arrival, Salerno was attacked by the Saracens,** Muslim Arabs from North Africa. These Muslims had already conquered the island of Sicily.

334. According to legend, while the Lombard prince agreed to the Saracen demands and decided to pay tribute, the Normans ridiculed him, sallying out and defeating the Saracen raiders.

335. The prince of Salerno, expressing his gratitude, offered the Normans to stay at his court and granted them lands. He even proposed that more people come from Scandinavia to join these settlements.

336. This led to a practice that is sometimes referred to as the "tradition of Salerno," with bands of Vikings regularly arriving in the Mediterranean to seek new opportunities.

337. **Other contemporary accounts dispute this story, but by the beginning of the 11th century,** the Vikings had established a small presence in southern Italy, which they would gradually expand over the decades.

338. Around the year 1020, **the Normans would join the local Lombard rulers in a rebellion against Byzantine control in the city of Bari.**

339. **The rebellion would end in a failure, with the Lombards unable to overthrow their Byzantine overlords.** However, the Viking warriors continued to enlist in local armies as mercenaries.

340. **About a decade later, Norman chief Rainulf gained lands in Aversa,** having helped a local prince against his rivals from Capua.

341. **The Norman chiefs were eventually able to expand their possessions.** In addition to the County of Aversa, they gained lands in Melfi and Capua, near the modern-day city of Naples.

342. **As they settled these lands, they adopted local Lombard culture** and assimilated themselves with the population, just as they had done in Normandy centuries before.

343. By the 1060s, **the Normans had established a permanent presence in southern Italy,** becoming a staple part of local armies and even beginning to extensively fight for the Byzantine emperor as part of **the Varangian Guard.**

344. **The Normans had not yet formed what we would call a "state," but their settlements were still closely interlinked.** Their control of the land was based on hereditary succession.

345. **Having established themselves in the region, the Normans regularly interacted with the papacy,** aiming to gain legitimacy by being endorsed by the pope. The pope's recognition would increase their status in the region.

346. **The Normans from the House of Hauteville managed to gain the title of count of Sicily,** which was under the suzerainty of the duke of Apulia, by the pope.

347. **However, Sicily was not yet in their control. The Normans launched an invasion of Sicily,** which was under Arab rule, in the 1060s.

348. **Roger de Hauteville managed to take the crucial city of Palermo in early 1072.**

349. **Roger I de Hauteville, a Norman from northern France with Viking origins,** became the first count of Sicily and continued the conquest of the island for the next few decades.

350. **The House de Hauteville continued its efforts to expand in mainland southern Italy.** Due to the waning presence of the Byzantines in the region, the Hautevilles were able to take over much of the former Byzantine territories.

351. **By 1091, the island of Sicily was completely under Norman control.** The Normans introduced Latin Christianity on a large scale to the island.

352. **With the agreement of Pope Innocent II, Roger II de Hauteville officially created the Kingdom of Sicily on Christmas Day,** 1130, which included the island, the Maltese archipelago (which the Normans had conquered in the late 11th century), and the lands of the former Duchy of Apulia, which had also been controlled by the Normans.

353. **The Kingdom of Sicily was the second major state that was conquered by the Normans,** with England being the first.

354. **Unlike the campaign of William of Conqueror, which was successful soon after the victory at Hastings in 1066,** the conquest of southern Italy and Sicily was a much more lengthy and costly endeavor for the Normans.

355. All in all, **the Norman conquest of southern Italy** remains one of the most interesting and unique occurrences of **the Middle Ages.**

Viking Expansion
(793–1066)

Explore the fascinating history of Vikings in this chapter. We'll look at interesting facts about **Viking culture, raids, and religion,** among other things. Discover how their superior **navigational skills** allowed them to reach distant lands, and learn about famous warriors like **Ragnar Lodbrok.**

356. **The Vikings came from Scandinavia and were advanced seafarers and traders.**

357. **They traveled vast distances, often by sea, to establish trading routes throughout much of northern Europe and beyond.** However, they were also known for their daring and brutal raids.

358. **The term "Viking" originates from Old Norse, víkingr, which means "pirate" or "raider."**

359. **The Vikings initially raided other lands rather than establishing permanent settlements,** although they eventually settled in places like England and Scotland as the years passed.

360. By the late 8th century, **Viking expeditions had reached as far east as Constantinople and Baghdad in the Middle East and even into North Africa.**

361. **Vikings were well known for their daringness and curiosity to explore new places.** This led them to discover Iceland around 830.

362. **They were some of the first Europeans to explore North America. Leif Erikson** established a settlement in modern-day Newfoundland, Canada, in 1000, predating Christopher Columbus by about five hundred years!

363. **The height of Viking presence is often referred to as the Viking Age,** which lasted from the 8th to the 11th century.

364. **Vikings often raided coastal towns or monasteries along with undefended settlements.** They pillaged valuable resources like silver coins, gold jewelry, and religious artifacts, which could be traded for goods back home or used to pay off debts or tribute demands from foreign rulers.

365. **The raid on the Lindisfarne monastery in Northumbria,** England, in 793 is one of the first well-documented Viking raids.

366. **Initially, the Vikings were pagans.** They had their own pantheon of gods and a very interesting mythology.

367. **Norse mythology features numerous gods, such as the thunder god Thor and the fertility goddess Freyja,** and interesting stories, including one about the end of the world (Ragnarök).

368. **Vikings increasingly embraced Christianity in the 10th century after they had been exposed to the religion during their travels and raids in European lands.**

369. **Ragnar Lodbrok is one of the most well-known Viking warriors. In 845,** he attempted to attack Paris but failed. Despite this, his reputation among other warriors grew until his death at the hands of **King Aella of Northumbria** in 865.

370. **The main reason the Vikings spread so quickly across Europe was that they possessed superior navigational skills.** They had intricate star maps, used constellations and celestial bodies to guide the way, and knew about ocean currents and winds.

371. In 970, **Norway and Denmark were united under a powerful Viking named King Harald Bluetooth of Norway.**

372. **Vikings were renowned for their ferociousness and strength.** They were brilliant warriors who excelled at close combat.

373. **Viking mercenaries were often employed by other kings in their armies.** The Byzantine Empire, for example, had a Viking contingent in its army for a long time.

374. **Most Viking warriors used the bearded ax during raids.** These axes had long handles and double-edged blades that could be used for both slashing and thrusting attacks while also being able to penetrate armor more effectively than swords.

375. **Many new techniques for shipbuilding were developed during the Viking Age, including the**

376. **use of iron nails instead of wooden pegs,** which made ships more seaworthy.

377. **The Vikings were able to travel farther afield and reach new lands** with relative ease compared to other Europeans, who were limited by their own technological and navigational capabilities.

378. **The Vikings were not only raiders.** They also developed trading routes around Europe, especially in the Baltic Sea area.

379. **Birka** (modern-day Sweden) **was a major center for trade in Scandinavia.** Traders dealt in furs, fish, timber, and slaves.

380. By 922, **the Vikings had established settlements along much of northern Europe's coastline,** including York/Jorvik (England), Dublin (Ireland), and Normandy (France), among others.

381. **Christianity spread throughout northern Europe in the 11th century and caused religious tensions between those Vikings who kept the Norse gods and those who had converted.** This led to increased hostility between groups, which eventually resulted in the decline of raiding fleets.

382. **The Vikings also impacted culture. They brought new words and ideas to the English language,** such as "Tuesday" (from Tiwesdæg) and "Thursday" (from Þórsdagr), as well as phrases like "berserk," which comes from Old Norse berserkr, meaning "bear-shirt" or a warrior wearing bearskin armor.

383. **The most successful Viking raiders were often referred to as berserkers.** They would go into a trance-like state during battle to increase their strength and ferocity.

384. The longship was vital to successful Viking expeditions. These vessels could be rowed by oarsmen or sailed depending on conditions, making them ideal for raiding coastal towns or quickly traveling far distances without relying solely on the wind.

385. There are many theories on why the Vikings decided to expand. One of the most popular theories suggests that Scandinavia experienced a population boom, and there was a shortage of food.

386. Other explanations include the advanced nature of their naval technology, which incentivized exploration and naval travel. Political and economic ambitions also might have played a role.

387. Vikings were colonizers in some lands, such as in eastern Europe and modern-day Ukraine and Russia. The first state-like formations in these regions emerged after the arrival of the Vikings, who conquered the local peoples and exacted tribute from them.

388. Kievan Rus, for example, the state centered around the city of Kiev (now spelled as Kyiv), was founded by a Viking named Rurik.

389. The Viking Age ended in 1066 when King Harald Hardrada of Norway was defeated at **the Battle of Stamford Bridge** by **the Anglo-Saxon forces led by Harold Godwinson.**

390. Although Viking expansion ended, the Vikings' legacy still lives on today through art, literature, and media. Many people worldwide continue to be fascinated by these fierce warriors and their incredible feats that have been immortalized in history.

Kievan Rus'
(9th–13th centuries)

Explore the history of Kievan Rus', one of the most interesting and earliest eastern European states **in the Middle Ages.** Find out more about its founding and what led to it becoming one of the most prosperous **Orthodox kingdoms.** Learn about important rulers **like Prince Vladimir and Yaroslav the Wise.** There is much to unpack here, so let's get started!

391. **Kievan Rus', which was established in the 9th century, was founded by Scandinavian Vikings.**

392. **The Vikings ventured deep into eastern Europe and settled in the region that would become Kiev,** the capital of the Rus'.

393. **Kievan Rus' was founded by a Viking named Rurik,** who established the Rurik dynasty.

394. **The Rurik dynasty ruled Kievan Rus' for more than seven hundred years,** with various branches holding power in different parts of the realm.

395. **Kiev quickly became one of the centers of eastern Europe due to its convenient location on the Dnieper River.** The city connected the northern peoples of Scandinavia with the Black Sea and the Byzantine Empire through trade

396. **Princess Olga of Kiev, a ruler in the 10th century, was one of the first recorded royals in the region to convert to Christianity in 957,** laying the groundwork for the Christianization of Kievan Rus'.

397. In 988, **Prince Vladimir the Great of Kiev formally embraced Christianity and ordered the mass baptism of his subjects in the Dnieper River,** marking a pivotal moment in the Christianization of the region.

398. **As Kievan Rus' flourished as a key trading hub between the Byzantine Empire and the northern European countries,** the kingdom accumulated wealth. It also was the recipient of cultural exchange.

399. Since **the Byzantine Empire had more influence over Kievan Rus' than Rome did,** this early Russian kingdom converted to Orthodox Christianity instead of Catholicism.

400. **The military and social structure of Kievan Rus'** was characterized by a warrior aristocracy known as the boyars, who held significant political power and often commanded armies in times of conflict.

401. **The social hierarchy in Kievan Rus' was structured, with the grand prince at the top,** followed by the boyars, lesser nobility, merchants, and peasants. This hierarchy extended to the military, with the grand prince being the supreme commander.

402. **Kievan Rus' employed a feudal-like system where the prince granted lands to the boyars and other nobles** in exchange for their military service and loyalty.

403. **The druzhina was a retinue of armed warriors who served the prince.** These loyal companions formed the core of the prince's military force and provided protection and support in times of war and peace.

404. **A code of honor and ethics known as druzhina duty guided the behavior of the warrior class.** This code emphasized loyalty to the prince, courage in battle, and hospitality to fellow warriors.

405. **Warfare was a significant part of Kievan Rus' society,** and the nobility prided themselves on their martial skills.

406. **Training in combat and horsemanship was a crucial part of the upbringing of young nobles.**

407. **Embracing their Viking heritage, the Rus' organized different sea raids** on neighboring territories, even reaching the Caspian Sea and Constantinople.

408. **In the face of constant threats from neighboring peoples, Kievan Rus' constructed a network of strategic fortresses,** such as the kremlins, to defend against external invasions and internal uprisings.

409. **Important military and political agreements were often sealed with feasts and oaths,** where leaders would share a communal meal and make solemn promises.

410. **The Kievan Rus' military strategy heavily emphasized the defense of the kingdom's vast territories,** using rivers, swamps, and dense forests as natural barriers against invading forces.

411. **Kievan Rus' warriors were skilled raiders, conducting hit-and-run tactics against neighboring territories.** These raids not only brought wealth but also tested their prowess and provided training.

412. **Warriors from Kievan Rus' would often be used as mercenaries by other states,** most notably the Byzantine Empire.

413. **An elite military unit that originated from Kievan Rus' and would be used extensively by the Byzantine rulers was the Varangian Guard.** This was how the Byzantines referred to the Norse Viking warriors.

414. **Overall, the relationship between Kievan Rus' and the Byzantine Empire was marked by both cooperation and rivalry,** resulting in diplomatic marriages, cultural exchanges, and territorial disputes.

415. **For example, the adoption of Orthodox Christianity linked Kievan Rus' to the Byzantine world,** resulting in the establishment of religious and cultural ties that persisted for centuries. However, the two states would also often contest each other for the control of trading routes.

416. **One of the most notable rulers of Kievan Rus' was Yaroslav I,** also known as **Yaroslav the Wise**, who ruled from 1019 to 1054. His reign was marked by legal reforms, the promotion of education, and the development of a written legal code called **the Russkaya Pravda.**

417. **Kievan Rus' saw a flourishment of artistic and architectural achievements,** with impressive structures such as **the Saint Sophia Cathedral in Kiev,** which is considered one of the finest examples of Byzantine architecture in eastern Europe.

418. **The death of Yaroslav the Wise led to political fragmentation and internal strife among his descendants,** contributing to the weakening and eventual fragmentation of Kievan Rus' into smaller principalities.

419. **In 1240, Kievan Rus' fell to the Mongol invasion led by Batu Khan,** marking the end of its autonomy and the beginning of the Mongol domination known as the Tatar yoke.

420. **The Tatar Yoke would last for almost two and a half centuries until the Russian princes** were able to defeat their Mongol suzerains in the 15th century.

421. **The Mongols emerged as political overlords of the former princes,** who had to formally legitimize their titles with visits to the Mongol khans in the Golden Horde.

422. **Despite the Mongol rule, Kievan Rus' left a lasting impact on the formation of Russian identity,** language, and culture, shaping the foundation for the later Russian state.

423. **While not exclusive to Kievan Rus', slavery was present,** with slaves serving as laborers, servants, and even warriors.

424. **Becoming a warrior was marked by rituals and ceremonies. Young nobles would receive their weapons and armor,** often as gifts from their families, symbolizing their entry into the ranks of the warrior class.

425. **Ivan the Terrible, the first official tsar of Russia, claimed a connection to Kievan Rus'** to legitimize his rule and strengthen his ties to its historical legacy.

426. **Alongside Kiev, other cities like Novgorod and Chernigov** (now known as Chernihiv) emerged as important economic centers, playing crucial roles in trade, governance, and cultural exchange.

427. **After the fall of Kiev, Novgorod would be one of the first independent city-state republics in Europe,** being ruled by a council.

428. **Kievan Rus' saw the development of a distinctive literature,** including religious texts, chronicles, and epic poetry.

429. **The legal and administrative innovations of Kievan Rus',** such as the division of the realm into principalities and the council of nobles known as the veche, had a lasting impact on subsequent Russian governance.

430. **The historical legacy of Kievan Rus' continues to influence modern nations, such as Russia, Ukraine, and Belarus,** shaping their historical narratives, cultural identity, and geopolitical dynamics.

Feudalism
(9th–14th centuries)

Feudalism was a social, political, and economic system that changed Europe. This section will explore how it evolved through medieval times and how it worked.

431. **The Feudal system started to emerge from about the 9th century,** reaching its peak during the High Middle Ages and entering a slow period of decline from the 14th century onwards.

432. **It was a hierarchical system of social organization,** where the king stood at the top, followed by ranks of social strata based on land ownership.

433. **Feudal society had three main classes: nobles, clergymen/clerics, and peasants or serfs.** Each class had a specific role within society.

434. **At its core, feudalism was based on the relationship between a vassal** (a peasant or a person of lower social standing) and his lord or suzerain.

435. **The lord (a person of higher social standing) granted a fief (land) to his vassals,** who provided him with loyalty and military support in times of need in exchange for that land grant, known as feudal tenure or fiefdom.

436. **Vassals promised to serve their liege lord by taking an oath called an homage.** This was like a contract, as it created a legal bond between them as master and servant.

437. **The manor system developed out of this arrangement,** which allowed peasants access to the lord's lands while living off of those lands themselves.

438. **This arrangement had its origins in the ancient Roman villas,** a system of lavish estates whose patrician owners designated different plebeians to administer and work their lands for them in return for accommodation and a small income.

439. **The primary source of income for feudal lords came from taxes collected by peasants working on their land.** The lord would use this money to pay for military campaigns or build fortifications.

440. In return for their loyalty, **vassals were allowed to keep some of the harvested crops from that land** and any profits made through its sale or trade.

441. **Feudalism included subinfeudation, where one manor could be split into smaller pieces.** These pieces were held by different families who belonged to various levels in the social hierarchy. Obligations between the families ran up and down like an inverted pyramid structure.

442. **The eldest son inherited most lands under primogeniture laws.** Younger sons had limited rights, so many became priests or joined a religious order or the military.

443. **Women had limited rights under feudalism but could still own property, manage households,** and inherit titles from their fathers if they didn't have any brothers. However, these instances were very rare, and in most cases, women who inherited property still depended on men to help fulfill the call for military service.

444. **Since most economic and political power was concentrated in the hands of a small number of lords,** the feudal system encouraged the building of provincial centers around the lords' dwellings, around which small towns and farmlands would emerge.

445. **The church played an important role in feudal society since it had its own set of laws that were separate from those governing secular matters.** Disputes between nobles could often be settled more quickly if they were brought before a bishop or other religious official.

446. **Theoretically, feudalism was based on the idea of mutual obligation between lords and their vassals,** with each one having certain rights and responsibilities to uphold in exchange for loyalty and protection from the other.

447. **In reality, however,** the powerful lords often cared less about the rights of the peasants and abused them.

448. **Knighting ceremonies were held during this period to honor vassals who showed exceptional loyalty and bravery in battle.** Their lord gave them a special sword, shield, and spurs as symbols of their allegiance.

449. **Knights were expected to adhere to a code of chivalry.** They had certain privileges, such as being allowed into noble courts and taking high-ranking positions in armies.

450. **Tournaments were held regularly throughout Europe during medieval times.** These events showcased a knight's combat skills while providing entertainment and gambling, making them very popular with the nobility, royalty, and commoners.

451. **Feudalism was based on hereditary rights, meaning that land would be passed from one family to the next.** If someone died without an heir, their land could become available for other nobles or peasants to claim, depending on their power.

452. **Kings were on top of the feudal system and owned the most lands,** making them the most powerful and important figures in the kingdom.

453. **During the peak of the High Middle Ages,** the Feudals had managed to emerge as the most powerful class throughout Europe, with kings heavily relying on their support in order to gain legitimacy and, therefore, indirectly strengthening the system.

454. **Eventually, upset populations around Europe noticed that kings had virtually limitless power and would protest to gain more rights and check the sovereign's power.**

455. **In England, the Magna Carta** (1215) limited the king's power by establishing certain rights for barons and freemen while also making taxation fairer. It is considered one of the most critical documents in feudal history since it began limiting monarchical power.

456. **Toward the end of feudalism, the middle class started to emerge.** These people were neither peasants nor nobles; they dwelled in cities and often had their own private businesses or other lucrative professions.

457. **The gradual decline of feudalism coincides with increased levels of urbanization in Europe.**

458. **The middle class, which was mostly composed of merchants initially,** eventually accrued a lot of power in many European societies, rising to the top of the hierarchy.

459. **This was most apparent in places like northern Italy, like Genoa and Venice,** where feudal lords were replaced by a class of rich merchant oligarchs by the 1200s.

460. **France would be one of the first places where feudalism would be legally abolished,** doing so in 1789 during the French Revolution.

The Holy Roman Empire
(800/962–1806)

At times, the Holy Roman Empire was one of the most influential medieval states. Discover how it started and why it was able to obtain so much power with these fascinating facts.

461. Some scholars believe **the Holy Roman Empire was established when Pope Leo III crowned Charlemagne as emperor of the Romans on Christmas Day** in 800, as it symbolized the revival of the Roman imperial title in western Europe.

462. Others argue that **the Holy Roman Empire did not really emerge as its own sovereign political entity until about 150 years later, during the reign of Otto I.**

463. **Otto I's rule of the Holy Roman Empire** (r. 962–973) marked a significant phase in the empire's history, as he restored the concept of a strong centralized monarchy and developed close ties with the church.

464. **During Otto I's reign, the Holy Roman Empire began to be roughly organized in a way that would persist for centuries to come,** mostly in modern-day Germany and Austria.

465. **The Battle of Lechfeld** (955), **where Otto I defeated the Magyars,** solidified his power and halted the Magyar incursions into the empire.

466. **The Ottonian dynasty, which followed the reign of Otto I,** promoted a cultural revival known as **the Ottonian Renaissance.** This renaissance was characterized by artistic patronage, manuscript production, and architectural achievements.

467. **The Ottonian Renaissance was a time of stability and strength for the Holy Roman Empire,** during which significant efforts were made to spread Christianity in the pagan lands of modern-day eastern Germany.

468. Despite this, **the Holy Roman Empire would soon become the single most disorganized and decentralized state in Europe,** consisting of hundreds of small political formations that were only vaguely connected with each other and exercised relatively high levels of autonomy.

469. **This disintegration would come gradually and would be a result of quick territorial expansion to the east, as well as multiple wars with Italian and Frankish states.** Because of these wars, there were constant power changes.

470. Still, **the status of the Holy Roman emperor was very respected in Europe during the Early Middle Ages** due to its close connections to the papacy and historical ties from the time of Charlemagne.

471. **The Holy Roman emperors started to regard themselves as successors of the Western Roman Empire,** something that was far from reality.

472. **The quest for dominance and power resulted in the Investiture Controversy (1075–1122),** a struggle between **the Holy Roman emperors** and the papacy over the appointment of bishops and church officials. This conflict highlighted the tensions between secular and religious authority.

473. **Emperor Henry IV's journey to Canossa in 1077, where he stood barefoot in the snow to seek Pope Gregory VII's forgiveness,** symbolized the complex relationship between emperors and popes.

474. **The Concordat of Worms resolved the Investiture Controversy in 1122** by granting secular rulers the right to invest bishops with temporal authority while allowing the church to invest them with spiritual authority.

475. **From 1138 to 1252, the empire would be ruled by the Hohenstaufen dynasty,** which included emperors like Frederick Barbarossa and Frederick II, who sought to expand their influence across the Italian Peninsula, leading to more conflicts with the papacy.

476. **During this time, the Hohenstaufen rulers would regularly take part in the Crusades to expand their standing in the Christian world,** though most of their endeavors would yield no real results.

477. **Frederick II's involvement in Italian affairs led to his control over the Kingdom of Sicily** and his efforts to assert imperial authority in both northern and southern Italy.

478. **The defeat of Frederick II's heirs by the Papal States and other Italian forces** led to the decline of the Hohenstaufen dynasty and the fragmentation of imperial power.

479. The interregnum following the death of Frederick II (1254–1273) was a period of political chaos characterized by a lack of strong central authority.

480. During the interregnum, the empire's political structure was heavily decentralized, leading to many small provinces, baronies, duchies, and independent cities pursuing great political autonomy.

481. The Golden Bull of 1356, issued by Emperor Charles IV, established the electoral system for choosing the Holy Roman emperor, solidifying the role of seven electors who represented the various territories within the empire.

482. The Imperial Diet, a legislative assembly, played a key role in decision-making within the empire, allowing different territories to discuss matters of common interest.

483. Though the emperor was technically elected, not all territories of the empire had the right to vote.

484. The Imperial Diet only consisted of the most important and powerful provinces and duchies, like Bohemia or Austria, which were ruled by powerful families.

485. Dynastic rivalries emerged among noble families, which vied for control over territories and attempted to assert their claims to the imperial throne.

486. Many cities within the empire gained independence and imperial immediacy, an official mandate that placed them under the direct authority of the emperor and no one else, allowing them to govern themselves more effectively.

487. During this period, the Hanseatic League started to emerge, playing a significant economic role within the empire.

488. Despite the empire's political challenges, its territories experienced economic prosperity, with trade routes connecting various regions and contributing to cultural exchange. The Holy Roman Empire was one of the most prosperous empires in Europe.

489. The House of Luxembourg, which controlled the Duchy of Luxembourg and also Bohemia, Moravia, and other eastern territories, produced several emperors, including Charles IV.

490. In 1440, the throne of the emperor would be continuously occupied by the House of Habsburg until the Holy Roman Empire's dissolution by Napoleon in the 19th century.

491. **The Habsburgs came from the Duchy of Austria and eventually emerged as the most powerful ruling dynasty in Europe,** perhaps in all of history.

492. **They increased their status and power through an intricate web of alliances and marriages in the Late Middle Ages,** which led to members of the Habsburg family becoming powerful political figures in kingdoms throughout Europe.

493. **A great example of this was Charles V, who ascended the throne of the Holy Roman Empire in 1519.** He also inherited the throne of Spain and the lordship of the Netherlands through his Dukedom of Burgundy.

494. **Charles's dominions also included lands in northern Italy and the Kingdom of Naples,** as well as overseas territories obtained during the Spanish conquest of the Americas.

495. **The Diet of Worms of 1495 laid the foundations for a comprehensive political and legislative reform of the Holy Roman Empire.** It introduced an empire-wide tax and the Imperial Chamber Court, the empire's highest judicial institution.

496. **During the Renaissance, the Holy Roman Empire faced challenges in managing religious diversity due to the presence of Catholics, Lutherans,** and other religious groups, leading to conflicts and negotiations.

497. **The Peace of Augsburg in 1555 recognized the principle of cuius regio, eius religio,** which allowed individual rulers within the empire to choose either Lutheranism or Catholicism as the official religion of their territories.

498. **The Reformation caused even more fragmentation and the emergence of distinct regional identities within the empire's borders,** making the Holy Roman Empire even more difficult to govern.

499. **The Thirty Years' War, which was primarily fought within the empire's territories,** devastated much of central Europe and had lasting political and religious consequences, including the weakening of the empire, which started to lose its political power in the coming centuries.

500. **All in all, the Holy Roman Empire was a very complex and compelling political entity of medieval Europe,** which managed to exist for about one thousand years and influenced the social, economic, cultural, and political makeup of the continent throughout and after its existence.

The Great Schism
(1054)

The Great Schism of 1054 marked a decisive break in Christian history, dividing the church into two branches: Roman Catholicism and Eastern Orthodoxy. Let's explore what led to the schism and how it affected Europe.

501. **The Great Schism is sometimes called the East-West Schism or simply the Schism of 1054.**

502. **The Great Schism broke the ties between Eastern and Western Christianity,** resulting in two branches of Christianity: the Roman Catholic Church (Western) and the Eastern Orthodox Church (Eastern).

503. **This rift in the Christian religion still exists today,** although it is not as hostile as it once was.

504. **Before the Great Schism, the five holy sees of Christianity—Rome, Constantinople, Antioch, Alexandria, and Jerusalem—each had their own heads or patriarchs.**

505. **These holy sees were each equal to each other but were superior to others,** accruing great power and influence.

506. **After the loss of Alexandria, Jerusalem, and Antioch to the Muslims, Rome and Constantinople** became rivals with each other.

507. **The rivalry between Rome and Constantinople was caused by a long-standing disagreement over papal authority,** doctrine, and practices, as well as linguistic and cultural differences between the Latin-dominated West and the Greek East.

508. **The differences between Rome and Constantinople would increase over the centuries. In the 11th century,** these issues would formally escalate to a new level.

509. **The Church of Rome saw itself as the natural successor to the Western Roman Empire after its fall in 476.** Because of the institution's influence, the instability in Europe after the barbarian invasions, the power vacuum that existed, and the lack of communication with Constantinople, **the Roman Church** gained a lot of power, especially after crowning Charlemagne as the new emperor in 800.

510. **One important difference between Rome and Constantinople was the issue of papal primacy—the question of whether or not the bishop of Rome** (the pope) held supreme and universal power over the Christian Church.

511. **There were also theological issues, such as the question of the Filioque** (whether or not the Holy Spirit comes from both God the Father and Jesus).

512. **In 1053, the conflict would be accelerated when Patriarch Michael Cerularius I of Constantinople** criticized the Latin practices of using unleavened bread during the Eucharist and forced the Latin churches in Constantinople to conduct mass in Greek.

513. As a response, in 1054, **Pope Leo IX sent three cardinals to Constantinople bearing a papal bull excommunicating Michael Cerularius and his followers,** who refused Communion with Rome.

514. This move was seen as provocative by the Eastern Church, **leading to Patriarch Michael I Cerularius of Constantinople excommunicating Leo IX and his followers.**

515. **Western Europe would officially fall under the direct influence of the bishop of Rome** (the pope), while eastern Europe and other lands of **the Byzantine Empire** would fall under the influence of the patriarch of Constantinople.

516. **The Eastern Orthodox Church still believes the bishop of Rome has no more authority than any other bishop in Christendom.** The Roman Catholic Church asserts that the pope has "supreme and full primacy over the universal church."

517. **During the time of the Great Schism, Orthodox Christianity** is believed to have had more followers, although the majority was slim.

518. **The rift resulted in both sides creating distinct liturgies and practices,** including different forms of baptism and holy orders.

519. Political tensions emerged between the two camps, which can be seen during the Crusades when Catholics sacked Constantinople in 1244.

520. Though most Christians were unaware of the exact differences between the churches at the time, a sense of distrust slowly grew as time went by.

521. This split had significant implications for art and architecture, as each side developed a distinct style throughout history, such as frescoes and stained glass windows in Western Christianity.

522. Today, **many Eastern churches claim that the Ecumenical Patriarchate of Constantinople,** one of the fifteen autocephalous (self-governing) churches that make up the Eastern Orthodox Church, is the successor to the Supreme Patriarchate of Constantinople.

523. Since Constantinople (now Istanbul) holds a special cultural and historical importance, the see that is located there is considered to be the "first among equals" of all **Orthodox churches.** Its patriarch is considered to be the de facto leader and representative of **Eastern Orthodoxy.**

524. There have been multiple attempts at reconciliation throughout history by various popes and patriarchs, but none have succeeded so far due to deep-rooted theological disagreements on topics like papal supremacy and infallibility.

525. Pope Paul VI met Patriarch Athenagoras I in 1965 during the Second Vatican Council, where they both agreed to lift the excommunications on each other and called for unity among Christians.

The Norman Conquest of England
(1066)

The Norman Conquest fundamentally shifted the people's way of life in England and beyond. Let's take a look at how the Norman conquest came about and how it impacted the country.

526. The Anglo-Saxon era of English control came to an end in 1066 with the invasion of William of Conqueror, Duke of Normandy.

527. The Duchy of Normandy had been created in 911 when King Charles III of West Francia allowed a group of Vikings, under the warlord Rollo, to settle in the northern part of modern-day France on the coast of the English Channel.

528. The Treaty of Saint-Clair-sur-Epte, which was signed in 911, officially established Rollo as duke in exchange for his loyalty to the French king and the promise that he would defend the French lands from other Viking raids.

529. What followed was decades of assimilation. Rollo and his people adopted French customs and converted to Christianity, eventually emerging as one of the most powerful duchies in Francia.

530. In fact, the name Normandy is derived from a combination of old Germanic words that mean "north" and "man." Many Europeans sometimes referred to all Vikings as Normans (though the term essentially means the descendants of Rollo from Normandy).

531. In 1042, Edward the Confessor, the descendant of Athelstan, succeeded to the throne of England from the son of Cnut the Great, Harthacnut, restoring the control of the House of Wessex.

532. He managed to take the throne with the support of the Normans. He was the son of Emma of Normandy, who married King Aethelred and then King Cnut. Aethelred had been ousted by King Cnut in 1016.

533. Edward lived in Normandy his whole life and was supported by the local nobles. He repaid them generously once he was able to win back the throne of England by appointing them to powerful positions.

534. However, when Edward the Confessor died in 1066, he left no clear heirs to succeed to the throne of England.

535. The closest male relative he had was Harold Godwinson, Earl of Wessex, who was the most powerful English noble who came from an established dynasty.

536. Harold would be elected king after the death of Edward by the Witan, the advisory council to the king.

537. Harold's legitimacy was instantly challenged by two different powerful figures who believed they had a claim to the throne of England.

538. The first challenger to the throne was William, Duke of Normandy, who was Edward the Confessor's first cousin once removed.

539. William claimed that Edward had personally appointed him his successor in secret. He set out to take the throne by force and was supported by the Norman nobility in England and Normandy.

540. The other claimant was the king of Norway, Harald Hardrada, who claimed the throne through his father, Magnus the Good, who had planned to restore Viking rule in England after the death of Harthacnut in 1042.

541. These complex circumstances led to three powerful figures all claiming the right to the throne of England, leading to one of the most exciting and impactful events of the Middle Ages.

542. The first to strike would be Harald Hardrada, who landed in northern England with three hundred ships. He led an army of about fifteen thousand men.

543. Harald Hardrada was assisted by Earl Tostig Godwinson, the brother of King Harold, who had his own ambitions of dethroning his brother.

544. On September 20th, 1066, the Norwegian force defeated the English resistance at the Battle of Fulford and went on to take the city of York, which surrendered without putting up a fight.

545. A few days later, King Harold confronted the triumphant Norwegians near Stamford Bridge. The English emerged victorious in this decisive battle, with both King Harald Hardrada and Tostig dying.

546. The victory was very costly. According to legend, a lone Dane held up the entirety of the English army at the bridge, preventing them from crossing and allowing the Norwegian army to organize itself since it had been caught by surprise.

547. The surviving Vikings were forced to accept a truce with the English and left the island. But King Harold had little time to celebrate his victory, as William of Normandy had begun his offensive in the south.

548. William of Normandy assembled a rather large force, though the exact number is disputed due to the unreliability of contemporary sources. The number of ships goes as high as 750.

549. The army, which contained contingents from different French provinces, had been assembled in August but had to wait for favorable winds to cross the English Channel.

550. The Normans landed in Sussex right as King Harold defeated the Norwegians at Stamford Bridge.

551. The Normans erected a wooden fortress at Hastings, which they used as a base camp to raid the neighboring countryside.

552. King Harold was forced to rush south after his costly victory at Stamford Bridge. He likely had around eight thousand men, none of whom had a proper chance to rest.

553. **The two sides clashed at Hastings on October 14th,** 1066. After a long battle, the Normans emerged victorious, having utilized their cavalry to break the enemy and kill the English king.

554. From then on, **the Normans had a relatively easier time conquering England.** They were able to quell resistance by local lords by December of 1066.

555. **On Christmas Day, 1066, William, who would come to be known as William the Conqueror,** was crowned king at Westminster Abbey in London. His coronation at the abbey would set a precedent for later English monarchs.

556. **Despite William's coronation, he had to fight to consolidate his position as king for the next five years.** He had to deal with local rebellions and the raiding Vikings.

557. **William the Conqueror gradually reorganized the administrative system by placing loyal Normans in positions of power.**

558. **William conducted the court in Norman French,** which greatly affected the evolution of the English language.

559. **The Domesday Book was created during William's reign.** This survey allowed him to learn about land and wealth distribution to impose a comprehensive tax reform.

560. **The Norman Conquest of England remains one of the most impactful occurrences of the Middle Ages,** as it almost completely transformed the socio-political and cultural makeup of England and established a new dynasty.

Medieval France
(10th–14th centuries)

Now that we have talked about the Norman Conquest, let's take a look at what the region of France was up to during this time. Medieval France is a fascinating topic in and of itself, and these thirty interesting facts will shed some light on why.

561. **Charlemagne's conquests laid the foundations for the establishment of cohesive political structures** and states in western Europe.

562. **After the breakup of the Carolingian Empire with the Treaty of Verdun,** the lands of West Francia would eventually develop into the Kingdom of France.

563. **French state-building took multiple centuries** and was one of the most unique political processes of medieval Europe.

564. **The political system of West Francia and the later Kingdom of France was very decentralized.** The king's authority was derived largely from the amount of support he had from local dukes and nobles.

565. **A prominent example of this was the Duchy of Normandy, a culturally and ethnically different region,** which had a large degree of autonomy while nominally being loyal to the French king.

566. **In this political system, the seat of the French king was the populous and prosperous Île-de-France region,** which housed the de facto capital of the French state, Paris.

567. **When the final Carolingian king, Louis V, died in 987 without any apparent heirs,** the French nobility decided to elect Hugh from the House of Capet as his successor.

568. **Hugh Capet, a nephew of Otto the Great of East Francia** (he later became emperor of the Holy Roman Empire) and a descendant of Charlemagne through his son Pepin of Italy, established the Capetian dynasty. **This dynasty would rule France until 1328.**

569. **The reign of the Capetian kings marked the height of the decentralized political system.** The king's vassals acted independently for the most part and came together to support the king in times of need.

570. **This system helped accelerate the growth and influence of the feudal system in France.** Feudalism was the chief system of social organization in France for perhaps the longest time out of the western European nations.

571. **The Capetian kings fought repeatedly against their powerful vassals,** who sometimes came together to demand more rights from their overlords.

572. For example, **King Louis VI, who ruled from 1108 to 1137, was constantly engaged in domestic conflicts with local leaders,** known as the "robber barons," who challenged the king's authority and had large personal armies.

573. **Capetian kings later had to deal with another problem that posed a threat to their authority:** the rise of the Angevin Empire during the 12th and 13th centuries.

574. **The Angevin Empire refers to the possessions of the House of Plantagenet under English King Henry II,** who, through a complex series of succession disputes, was also the duke of Normandy, count of Anjou, and duke of Aquitaine.

575. **This meant a foreign monarch was virtually equal in status to the French king.** The English king was in control of a substantial portion of French fiefdoms that were under the vassalage of the French king. This created complications that resulted in a full-blown war between the Capetian and Angevin kings.

576. **The Angevin-Capetian rivalry lasted for about a century until 1259 when the Capetians finally emerged victorious after a long struggle.** With the Treaty of Paris, they regained possession of most of the Angevin lands.

577. **French King Philip II, the same king who embarked on the Third Crusade,** played a big part in the French victory over the Angevins during his reign from 1180 to 1223.

578. **He managed to lead his armies to military victories and also introduced a wide range of administrative and tax reforms.** He even built a defensive wall around Paris!

579. **For his efforts, a contemporary French chronicler gave him the name "Augustus,"** denoting the achievements of the king and equaling him in status with the Roman emperors.

580. Many historians argue that the developments during this large-scale conflict acted as a precursor to the more well-known **Hundred Years' War between France and England,** which began in 1337.

581. **The House of Capet also managed to strengthen the central monarchy,** something that would lead to the economic and military dominance of France in the coming centuries.

582. **Philip IV (r. 1285–1314) continued to reform France, most notably establishing the Parlement of Paris,** an appellate court that served as the judicial foundation for the establishment of a system of courts throughout the different provinces of France.

583. **Philip IV also confiscated possessions from and arrested the Knights Templar,** something that greatly enriched the crown.

584. **King Philip IV's reign saw the establishment of the Avignon Papacy.** The popes at Avignon were under French influence for about seventy years.

585. **The House of Capet would eventually be replaced with the House of Valois in the 14th century, leading to the outbreak of the Hundred Years' War.** This large conflict helped grow a sense of better-defined national identities in both France and England.

The Crusades
(1095–1291)

Starting in 1095, European powers launched a series of military campaigns known as the Crusades. Each campaign had a different goal, but they were all designed to promote **Christendom and stop the pagans from expanding.** This chapter will explore the events that took place during the Crusades, such as some of the major battles that were fought and how effective the Crusades ultimately were.

586. **The Crusades were launched by Christian European factions.** The Crusades that took place from 1095 to 1291 sought to take back holy sites in the Muslim-occupied Levant.

587. **Pope Urban II initiated the First Crusade with a speech at Clermont-Ferrand on November 27th, 1095, which called for Christian knights** to take up arms and march eastward to recover Jerusalem from Muslim rule.

588. **The armies of the First Crusade were made up mostly of French nobles but also included contingents from Germany, Italy, England, and Spain.** Some peasants joined this crusade out of religious fervor or economic desperation.

589. **The First Crusade would ultimately be successful,** reclaiming Jerusalem and a strip of land along the eastern Mediterranean coast by 1099.

590. **The Crusaders organized four Catholic Crusader States in the Holy Land: the Kingdom of Jerusalem, the Principality of Antioch, the County of Edessa, and the County of Tripoli.** Leaders of the Crusades emerged as rulers of the Crusader States, establishing hereditary rule.

591. **The Second Crusade was launched by European powers in 1145. It was led by King Louis VII of France** against Muslims primarily located around Damascus following the fall of the County of Edessa.

592. **The other significant leader of this crusade was Holy Roman Emperor Conrad III.** The leaders from the Crusader States also provided forces for the Second Crusade.

593. **The Second Crusade was a complete failure. Many died due to famine, disease, or battle.** It did not achieve its goals, and it also strained relations between European powers, which did not agree with each other during the campaign.

594. **The Third Crusade was launched in response to the Muslim recapture of Jerusalem in 1187.** The Fatimid Caliphate, under Saladin, had managed to rise to power and put pressure on the Crusaders in the Levant.

595. **The three leaders of the Third Crusade were Richard the Lionheart of England, Philip II of France,** and Frederick Barbarossa of the Holy Roman Empire.

596. **The Crusaders faced a lot of issues even before arriving in the Holy Land.** For instance, **Emperor Frederick Barbarossa** drowned in a river in Anatolia, forcing many of his soldiers to abandon the effort.

597. **The Third Crusade successfully enabled a three-year truce between Christian and Muslim forces,** allowing Christians to visit Jerusalem without fear of attack. However, the Crusaders did not regain much land from Saladin, as he remained the ruler of most of Palestine.

598. **Pope Innocent III wanted the Fourth Crusade to go directly to Jerusalem, but instead, it ended with the sacking of Constantinople** (the capital city of the Eastern Roman Empire) in 1204.

599. **The Crusaders ended up in a very complex situation after leaving their homes on the way to the Holy Land.** They did not have enough money to pay the Venetians for using their ships, so the Crusaders were at their whim.

600. The Fourth Crusade remains one of the most shameful events in the history of Christianity, as Catholic forces killed around two thousand civilians in Constantinople.

601. The sack of Constantinople significantly weakened the Byzantine Empire and ultimately led to its fall in 1453 at the hands of the Ottoman Turks.

602. The Fifth Crusade was led by King Andrew II of Hungary and Leopold VI of Austria against Muslim forces under Sultan al-Kamil, Saladin's nephew.

603. Other leaders included John of Brienne, a French knight who had been the king of Jerusalem; Oliver of Paderborn, a devout cleric who led Flemish and Dutch reinforcements that arrived later in the campaign; and Holy Roman Emperor Frederick II, who did not actually take part in the campaign despite his promise.

604. The Fifth Crusade was very disorganized. After some initial actions in the Levant, not much was accomplished. **King Andrew** returned home.

605. The Crusaders would go on to successfully capture the Egyptian port city of Damietta, holding it for two years, but they underestimated the Muslim forces. They would be expelled from the city in 1221.

606. An eight-year truce would be signed between the Muslims and what was left of the Crusaders in the Holy Land following the failure of the Fifth Crusade.

607. The Sixth Crusade would be launched in 1227. It was led by Frederick II of the Holy Roman Empire and would prove to be successful in reclaiming Jerusalem.

608. Holy Roman Emperor Frederick II met with the Ayyubid sultan, al-Kamil, and negotiated the peaceful cession of Jerusalem, as well as of some of its surrounding territories.

609. Frederick II would crown himself the new king of Jerusalem before sailing back to the Holy Roman Empire. He never stepped foot in the Holy Land again.

610. **The Seventh Crusade was launched by Pope Innocent IV in 1248 and was led by King Louis IX of France against Muslim forces under Sultan al-Malik Muhammad** in response to the loss of Jerusalem in 1244.

611. **The Seventh Crusade ultimately failed, with Louis IX being captured and later released after paying a large ransom.** This was seen as a humiliation for Europe's Crusader forces, who could not achieve their goals despite having some initial success.

612. **The Seventh Crusade was Europe's last attempt to launch military campaigns to reclaim the Holy Land from the Muslims.** The Europeans finally realized the Crusades were very expensive and difficult to maintain and ultimately fielded no good results in the long run.

613. **King Louis IX would launch the Eighth Crusade** in 1270, this time against the Muslim Hafsid dynasty in Tunisia.

614. **No land was won for the Christians, even though it started well.** Many believe this is because the Crusader armies were weakened by disease and hunger, making their chances of victory small.

615. **Other Crusades included campaigns launched against the Muslims in Iberia and pagans in eastern Europe.**

Catholic Military Orders

When looking at the Middle Ages, it is important to take a look at the many Catholic orders that exerted their influence, especially during the Crusades. Let's examine some facts about the Catholic orders, including the most influential ones and the rules they had to follow.

616. **Military orders were Christian societies of knights,** which began to be established during the era of the Crusades.

617. **The most prominent military orders were the Knights Templar, the Knights Hospitaller,** the Teutonic Knights, and the Knights of Santiago.

618. **These organizations were meant to defend the Christian populations and pilgrims and fight the Muslims and pagans.**

619. **Later on in their existence, they developed into powerful and self-sustaining entities that gained immense political power** and dominated states during the Middle Ages.

620. **The first of the military orders to emerge were the Knights Templar and the Knights Hospitaller in the 12th century.**

621. **Both organizations arose in the Levant after the success of the First Crusade and the establishment of the Crusader States.**

622. **The Knights Templar was founded around 1118 by a small group of knights led by Frenchman Hugues de Payens.**

623. **The knights pledged to defend the Christian pilgrims, who encountered problems on their way to the Holy Land** because of Muslim raiders.

624. **The Knights Templar were granted headquarters at the Mount Temple in the captured Al-Aqsa Mosque,** from where they continued to operate before the fall of Jerusalem.

625. **The Knights Hospitaller was initially part of a hospital designed to treat Christians in Jerusalem.**

626. The Knights Hospitaller were granted rights and possessions by the new Latin kings of Jerusalem and continued to operate their hospices in **the Holy Land** while also providing forces to fight against the Muslims.

627. These military orders lived by very strict guidelines. They followed a concrete set of rules and traditions, like celibacy, praying at certain times during the day, having communal dinners, participating in different rituals, and training.

628. They had a distinct hierarchy and were headed by the grand master. There were different ranks of high-standing individuals who each had their own separate responsibilities.

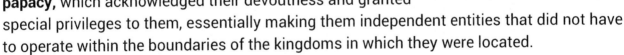

629. The Catholic military orders only accepted men, who were required to go through rigorous training to see whether they complied with the set of requirements. After serving in the lower positions in the orders (such as being squires), they eventually became knights.

630. The Templars and the Hospitallers were renowned in the Levant and later in Europe for their military prowess. They often constituted small, elite forces in the Crusader armies.

631. Unlike other soldiers of the time, they were always well equipped and had high discipline and morale, allowing the Crusaders to rely on their strength.

632. Eventually, the knights' services were appreciated by the rulers in the Holy Land. The orders were granted lands to organize their quarters, as well as strategic castles to help defend the Holy Land from the Muslims.

633. The military orders gained recognition from the papacy, which acknowledged their devoutness and granted special privileges to them, essentially making them independent entities that did not have to operate within the boundaries of the kingdoms in which they were located.

634. The military orders gathered a lot of wealth and power as time passed. Thousands of nobles donated riches, weapons, and valuables. They even voluntarily joined the orders in pursuit of glory and the belief that they were doing the right thing.

635. The military orders held many fortresses in the Levant, including Acre, Krak de Chevaliers, Tortosa, Beaufort, and Bagras. They also had fortifications throughout Europe, especially in France, England, and Iberia.

636. **Over time, new military orders began to emerge, such as the Knights of Santiago in Spain,** which helped the Christians in the Reconquista, and the Teutonic Order, which was first founded by German Crusaders in the Levant but ultimately moved its operations to the Baltic.

637. **However, with the decreasing power of the Crusader States,** they slowly began to lose their holdings in the Levant and were forced to relocate after the fall of Acre in 1291.

638. **The Knights Templar relocated to France, where they operated for about another thirty years before they were charged with a series of very serious allegations,** such as heresy, blasphemy, and corruption. The Templars were arrested in 1307.

639. **The final grand master of the Templar Order, Jacques de Molay, as well as hundreds of other brothers throughout France, were arrested.** Some were put on trial and even executed. Their possessions and estates were confiscated by the French Crown.

640. **The Templars were accused of engaging in heretical activities, such as spitting on the cross during their meetings,** indulging in carnal relations with other members, denying Christ, and worshiping different satanic idols.

641. **It is not exactly clear whether or not the Templars were guilty of the charges presented against them,** but they were arrested in other countries and forced to abandon their activities.

642. **As for the Hospitallers, they first relocated to Cyprus, then to Rhodes, and later to Malta after the fall of Acre.** They continued to conduct military operations, helping Christian factions fight against the Muslims.

643. **Unlike the Templars, they were never accused of similar crimes, but they continued to decline in importance as time went by. The Hospitallers** eventually abandoned their military activities but continued their civilian work.

644. **The Teutons relocated and were granted lands on the Baltic coast. From the 13th to the beginning of the 15th century,** they controlled a vast chunk of land and had their own state, fighting with the Catholics against the pagans before they declined after facing immense pressure from Poland-Lithuania, the Holy Roman Empire, and Russia.

645. **The Templars, Hospitallers, Teutons, and other Catholic military orders were a compelling and integral part of medieval military history.** Some of these orders, particularly the Templars, have a certain sense of mystery around them to this day.

Gothic Architecture
(12th–16th centuries)

Almost everyone has seen pictures of Gothic architecture, although some might not have realized it. One of the most famous is **Notre-Dame Cathedral** in France. Did you know it was built during the Middle Ages?

We'll take a look at interesting facts about Gothic architectural features and how stained glass artistry became famous. We will also discuss how the Gothic style inspired others to write novels or create amazing works of art.

646. **Gothic architecture is an architectural style that was very popular in Europe during the High and Late Middle Ages.**

647. **Gothic architecture emerged in France during the 12th century** and spread across Europe by the 16th century.

648. **Gothic architecture was a development of the Romanesque architectural style,** which was the most widespread in Europe after the fall of the Roman Empire.

649. **Gothic architecture is characterized by pointed arches,** ribbed vaults, flying buttresses, large windows, and spires or towers with multiple stories of diminishing size.

650. **The style was closely associated with cathedrals that were built to accommodate the increasing number of worshipers who embraced Christianity as their religion during this period.**

651. **The term "Gothic" was first used during the Renaissance.**

652. **The term originates from the Goths, the Germanic tribes that migrated to Europe** and eventually caused the decline of the Roman Empire.

653. **Renaissance writers used "Gothic" in a derogatory way.** The Renaissance promoted the classical style of doing things, which included architecture.

654. **Before that, the Gothic style was sometimes referred to as Opus Francigenum or "French Work."**

655. **Its popularity peaked between 1150 and 1530 and saw a revival from 1740 and 1860** during what is known as **the Neo-Gothic or Victorian Gothic Movement.**

656. **Chartres Cathedral, located southwest of Paris,** is considered an exemplary achievement in early Gothic design because its proportions are perfect according to mathematical calculations.

657. **It was built between 1194 and 1220 and stands on the site that had historically been the seat of the bishop of Chartres.**

658. **Notre-Dame de Paris is another famous example of Gothic architecture.** It began construction in 1163 and wasn't finished until 1260.

659. **During the French Revolution, Notre-Dame was destroyed.** It would not be restored until the mid-1840s. Interest in restoring this landmark was largely due to **Victor Hugo's book The Hunchback of Notre-Dame.**

660. **Gothic architecture was used for various structures, including churches, cathedrals,** monasteries, universities, and civic buildings, such as town halls.

661. **The pointed arches allowed for greater flexibility in the interior design by enabling it to be divided into several different levels,** with high ceilings giving more space for each level.

662. **The ribbed vaults and flying buttresses were introduced during this period.** These provided additional support to the walls while creating a visual effect that dramatically enhanced their appearance.

663. **Large windows filled the interiors with natural light,** and stained glass artistry became popular thanks to new glass-making technologies at this time.

664. **Spires or towers typically topped off these grandiose edifices,** which often reached up to three hundred feet tall.

665. **These soaring spires made impressive visual statements about the power and importance of religion.**

666. **They also served practical purposes, like acting as lightning rods,** which prevented the building from damage during thunderstorms.

667. **The combination of these elements allowed for larger window surfaces,** creating a more airy atmosphere within the interior compared to earlier Romanesque designs.

668. **Gothic architecture has been used in many countries across Europe,** including England, France, Germany, and Italy, with some variations depending on local traditions.

669. **The German Gothic style is characterized by its spires or towers and lack of interior decorations,** such as stained glass windows.

670. **The English Gothic style often features large rose windows filled with intricate patterns.**

671. **Italian architects combined elements from classical design to form a new style called Italian Gothic.** This style featured slender columns, round arches, and roofs that curved instead of having steep peaks like in other types of Gothic architecture.

672. **Using pointed arches made it possible to build higher towers,** allowing for better observation points when defense was necessary due to warring factions between countries or within them.

673. **Many large cathedrals took decades (or even centuries) to complete.**

674. **Constructing these grandiose buildings often required teams of highly skilled craftsmen working together** over many years before they could be considered finished.

675. **One example is Milan Cathedral,** which began construction around 1386 but wasn't completed until the 20th century when the final details on the exterior were added in 1965.

676. **Gothic architecture has been influential in modern buildings,** especially those built using steel frames rather than stone masonry.

677. **During the 19th century, the Gothic style became popular again due to its romantic associations with stories of chivalry.**

678. **Many castles were built during the Middle Ages using features like pointed arches and ribbed vaults.**

679. **Castles also added distinct touches like moats,** drawbridges, and fortified walls for extra protection against enemies that might try to invade.

680. **Stained glass windows were used to let light into dark interiors,** allowing people to see the beautiful scenes of biblical stories or saints' lives depicted on them.

681. **The pointed arch became a symbol of power for rulers who commissioned these structures.** It was often used in other forms of art, from paintings to sculptures, which helped spread its popularity throughout Europe.

682. **Architectural ornamentation was a vital part of creating visual appeal.** Carvings depicting biblical scenes or images of religious figures were popular choices among those who could afford them.

683. **Stone gargoyles were added at higher levels.** These were aesthetically pleasing and also provided additional protection against rainwater seeping into the walls below them by acting like drains.

684. **The Gothic style had a major effect on the arts, like music.** Composers like Bach and Handel wrote pieces that included features from cathedrals with pointed arches, ribbed vaults, and tall spires. This gave their works an impressive grandeur.

685. **Although Gothic architecture was initially resisted in some places for not fitting within traditional norms,** it eventually became widely accepted throughout Europe.

The Rise of Universities
(12th–15th centuries)

This chapter will explore the emergence of universities in Europe during the 12th and 15th centuries. We'll uncover exciting facts about their history, from their earliest foundations to how they adapted over the years. Let's take a look at how higher learning impacted the Middle Ages.

686. **The earliest European universities were established in Italy, France, England, Spain, Portugal, and Scotland.**

687. **The oldest university in Europe is believed to be the University of Bologna,** which opened in 1088. It is the oldest university in continuous operation.

688. **Oxford University is widely accepted as having been established around 1096.** Some argue that it wasn't a proper university at this time, but students were taught there beginning in 1096.

689. **Another important early European university was the University of Paris** (La Sorbonne), which was established in 1160.

690. **Universities were initially created to provide a place for scholars to study law,** medicine, philosophy, and theology outside religious institutions like monasteries and cathedrals.

691. **During this period, there was a great revival of learning known as scholasticism, which sought to reconcile Christian beliefs with classical Greek philosophies,** such as Aristotle's teachings on logic and natural sciences like biology, astronomy, and mathematics.

692. **Most schools were affiliated with religious orders, such as the Dominicans or Franciscans,** and education was primarily conducted in Latin.

693. **Medieval universities introduced a more formalized approach to teaching, learning, and research.**

694. **In 1450, Gutenberg's printing press revolutionized the dissemination of knowledge,** making books widely available at affordable prices.

695. **Early European universities served an essential role in society by providing legal and medical services to the local population.**

696. **Universities eventually provided a place for scholars to debate controversial topics,** such as religious beliefs, which helped lead to the Reformation in Europe during this period.

697. **Women were not generally allowed admission into early universities;** this would change increasingly in the 19th century.

698. **During this period, universities began to offer degrees and other forms of accreditation for those who completed their studies.**

699. **By 1400, most European universities had adopted some form of the examination process for admission into higher education institutions.**

700. **Early universities were largely independent of government control,** which allowed them more freedom when deciding how they taught subjects or what topics could be studied.

701. **Many famous figures attended medieval European universities, including Dante Alighieri** (Florence) and **Thomas Aquinas** (University of Naples).

702. **Some universities even began offering degrees in non-religious subjects like literature, music, or art,** allowing them to become hubs for creative thinkers across Europe.

703. **Universities also began hosting conferences that brought scholars from all over Europe** with different perspectives on philosophy, theology, and science.

704. **Early European universities often played an essential role in government** by helping train the next generation of leaders who could help guide their countries through turbulent times.

705. **The rise of universities during this period laid the foundation for modern higher education and helped to transform European society** into an increasingly scientific, intellectual, and progressive one.

The Inquisition
(12th–19th centuries)

This chapter will explore the disturbing history of the Inquisition, a series of Roman Catholic Church-led tribunals operating in Europe, Spain, and Portugal. We'll take a look at facts about their methods of interrogation, censorship laws, and how the Inquisition impacted Europe.

706. **There were multiple inquisitions in different countries, with the most famous occurring in Spain.** They lasted from the 12th to the 19th centuries, although they did not start and stop at the same time.

707. **The Roman Catholic Church led tribunals in Europe to identify any heresy among Christians.**

708. This practice had existed in **the Catholic world** in some shape or form before it became a more widespread and lasting institution in the 13th century.

709. In 1184, **Pope Lucius III sent bishops to southern France** to eliminate a group of heretics called the Catharists.

710. **The papacy also actively fought to eliminate groups of Waldensian believers in Italy** and Germany, a movement that was deemed to be heretical.

711. **Pope Gregory IX charged the Dominican and Franciscan Orders to track down heretics in 1231.** This was when an official court called the Inquisition was established.

712. **The Inquisition developed into a punitive measure against those accused of being witches or heretics.**

713. **It is likely that tens of thousands of individuals were executed by the Inquisition from the 12th century until the Catholic Church denounced the practice.**

714. **Interrogations conducted during the Inquisition included torture, arbitrary imprisonment without trial,** forced confessions under duress, and psychological coercion, such as sleep deprivation and starvation techniques.

715. **In 1474, Pope Sixtus IV sanctioned tribunals for Spain and Portugal;** this is often seen as the beginning of the Spanish Inquisition.

716. **One of the most widely notorious inquisitions was the Spanish Inquisition,** which began in 1478 and continued until 1834.

717. **The Spanish Inquisition was incredibly rigorous.** It involved a public ceremony where those convicted were paraded in front of an audience before being sentenced to death by burning at the stake.

718. **During the Spanish Inquisition's peak** (from 1480 to 1530), over two thousand people were executed due to their religious beliefs.

719. **Spain's Muslim population was among the most persecuted during the Spanish Inquisition,** as they were suspected of heresy and non-compliance with church doctrine.

720. **Muslims were forced to convert to Christianity** or faced expulsion from Spain. Thousands converted under duress but continued practicing their faith clandestinely, while many others left the country altogether.

721. **Jews were also targeted, especially Conversos** (those who had been forced to renounce **Judaism and accept Catholicism** but still practiced their faith in secret). It is believed that tens of thousands of Jews fled Spain during this time.

722. **In general, the inquisitions targeted anyone, whether they were nobles or peasants.** Anyone could be arrested if they were suspected of heresy, blasphemy, or witchcraft.

723. There are accounts from some inquisitors that indicate individuals who refused to confess could receive severely harsh punishments, such as having their tongues cut out or their limbs amputated.

724. The Roman Inquisition emerged in 1542 under Pope Paul III and lasted until the mid-18th century.

725. The Roman Inquisition's main focus was directed at combating Protestantism, which was quickly gaining traction in the 16th century.

726. In 1551, **Pope Julius III issued the papal bull Licet ab initio,** which granted inquisitors immunity from civil law when conducting their investigations.

727. The Inquisition was responsible for various cultural changes, including censorship laws that limited the spread of ideas about religion and philosophy, which, in turn, influenced Europe's views on science and learning.

728. One famous victim of the Spanish Inquisition was Miguel de Cervantes, who wrote Don Quixote.

729. Cervantes was arrested due to suspicion over his religious beliefs, and he was excommunicated and imprisoned.

730. Importantly, in most cases, the accused were not allowed to have legal representation, while it was very easy for the prosecution to prove their case – they only needed a confession by the accused.

731. Many famous scholars and scientists, including Galileo Galilei, found themselves targets during this period.

732. Galileo was interrogated multiple times over his support for Copernicus's theories on heliocentrism.

733. Galileo was tried in 1633 and found guilty of heresy, but instead of capital punishment, he was forced into house arrest for the rest of his life, and his works were censored.

734. **The Inquisition popularized the use of violence against anyone considered to be a heretic.** It is unknown how many people died by those who were not sanctioned by the Roman Catholic Church.

735. **This use of violence became evident during the infamous witch hunt period.** Many individuals were unlawfully prosecuted since they were believed to have been involved with witchcraft.

736. **Those facing judgment from an inquisitorial court were not given access to a lawyer** or allowed to present any witnesses in their favor.

737. **Between 1478 and 1834, it is believed that between sixty thousand and one hundred thousand individuals lost their lives during various inquisitions across Europe.** However, records from this period are incomplete, so the exact figure remains unknown.

738. **The Inquisition remains one of the most tragic and shameful parts of the history of the Catholic Church.**

739. **In some places, the Inquisition came to symbolize the church's immense power and influence,** and it also came to be associated with unnecessary evil and coercion.

740. In 1808, **Napoleon abolished all inquisitorial tribunals in Spain during his occupation. Ferdinand VII reestablished the Inquisition for a brief period.** It finally ended during **Queen Isabella II's** rule on July 15th, 1834.

Magna Carta
(1215)

Explore the fascinating history of the Magna Carta, and discover how its principles have formed a cornerstone in **modern constitutional democracies worldwide.** Learn what led to the forging of this document, and find out if it was as effective as history has made it out to be.

741. **The Magna Carta is considered to be the first document in European history that limits the power held by the monarch.**

742. **Originally, the document was drafted by Archbishop of Canterbury Stephen Langton** in an effort to make peace between **the English barons and King John I.**

743. **King John of England,** who had become very unpopular due to his treatment of the country's nobility, signed **the Magna Carta** on June 15th, 1215.

744. **The Latin name for the Magna Carta translates to "Great Charter."**

745. **In addition to limiting royal power, it also guaranteed certain liberties for English citizens,** making it a very important document for ordinary people.

746. **It was initially written in Latin because that was the language of the educated and the church elite.**

747. **Although the Magna Carta's original provisions have been amended over time, many still form part of UK law today,** including habeas corpus, which protects against unlawful detention without trial or charge.

748. **King John signed it under duress after his barons had captured London,** making him unable to exercise any power until he agreed to their terms.

749. **The charter was reissued thrice in 1216, 1217, and 1225,** with minor changes each time.

750. Later versions were issued by Edward I in 1297 as part of his reforms to English law, which became known as Confirmatio Cartarum, or Confirmation of Charters.

751. Only four original copies are believed to survive today. Two are held at the British Library, one at Salisbury Cathedral, and another at Lincoln Castle.

752. A copy from 1297 currently resides in the United States National Archives; it is one of four surviving original copies of the document that were issued after the death of King John.

753. The Magna Carta included sixty-three clauses that addressed different issues, such as royal taxation, feudal obligations, and baronial rights.

754. It states that no free man shall be arrested or imprisoned except by the legal judgment of his peers (other nobles) or according to a law established by the king.

755. It also stipulates that justice should not be sold, delayed, or denied and that widows cannot be forced to remarry against their will.

756. The charter was heavily criticized by some people at that time, mainly due to its protection for barons over commoners.

757. The original Magna Carta was not as influential as many think. It was annulled by Pope Innocent III in 1215, the same year it was issued.

758. The Magna Carta is one of the three most important charter documents from medieval England, with the other two being the Charter of Liberties (1100) and the Charter of the Forest (1217). These documents played a big role in solving legal disputes involving the king of England at the time.

759. As more progress was made toward equality and human rights in Europe, the Magna Carta started to be regarded as the "constitution" of England.

760. **The Magna Carta has become an icon of democracy, freedom, human rights,** and the rule of law throughout history. Its principles have been incorporated into many other constitutions around the world, including Japan, Canada, India, and New Zealand, among others.

761. **The charter has been widely used in political rhetoric throughout history to justify various causes,** such as the abolition of slavery in 19th-century America or people's right to self-rule during India's struggle against British colonialism.

762. **The Magna Carta has been an inspiration to many other charters,** such as the French Declaration of Rights in 1789, the US Bill of Rights in 1791, Brazil's Constitution of 1824, and South Africa's Freedom Charter in 1955.

763. **Lord Denning, an English jurist who became the King's Counsel in 1938, declared the Magna Carta "the greatest constitutional document of all time,** the foundation of the freedom of the individual against the arbitrary authority of the despot."

764. **The 800th-anniversary celebration took place in 2015. Queen Elizabeth II issued a statement reaffirming her commitment to upholding its core values.**

765. Regarded as one of the most important documents in history, **the Magna Carta is inscribed in UNESCO's Memory of the World Register.**

The Mongol Invasions and Conquest
(13th–14th centuries)

The Mongol invasions were an important period in history. The Mongols ended up conquering most of Eurasia, changing the lives of those who lived there. We'll look at **important Mongol leaders** and how they formed one of the largest empires in recorded history.

766. **The Mongol Empire would emerge after the unification of several nomadic tribes in modern-day Mongolia.**

767. **In 1206, a council would declare Genghis Khan as the Mongols' supreme leader,** beginning an era of Mongol expansion.

768. **The Mongol invasions would last for at least one hundred years** and would greatly influence the political, social, cultural, and economic state of Eurasia.

769. **The campaigns, which began under Genghis Khan,** resulted in the largest contiguous empire in world history.

770. **At its peak, it extended from eastern China to Poland.**

771. **During the invasions, millions of people were killed or enslaved by the Mongols.**

772. **The Mongols were known for their horsemanship skills, which helped them immensely when conquering vast lands quickly.** Their skills on horseback also allowed them to launch surprise attacks against enemies due to their mobility on battlefields.

773. **They were ruthless warriors and had a very strong sense of loyalty to their leaders,** like the strongest or most skilled military generals.

774. **During the invasions, Mongol armies were primarily composed of nomads from Mongolia** but also included soldiers from central Asia and even Europeans who defected or joined them voluntarily.

775. **The Mongols were known for their brutality in battle;** they often burned down entire cities and villages and massacred their inhabitants to demoralize those who opposed them.

776. **The Mongol invasions eventually led to the collapse of many existing empires, such as the Khwarezmian Empire** and **the Kievan Rus;** they also significantly weakened other states, like **the Byzantine Empire** and **the Abbasid Caliphate.**

777. **The Mongol Empire was divided into four parts after the death of Mongke Khan** (grandson of Genghis Khan) in 1294: the Ilkhanate, the Golden Horde, the Chagatai Khanate, and the Yuan dynasty.

778. **The Mongols first invaded China at the beginning of the 13th century. They decisively defeated the Chinese Jin dynasty at the Battle of Yehuling** in 1211, allowing them to penetrate into northwestern China and eventually subdue the Jin dynasty.

779. **The Mongol invasion of China would last for about seventy years before Kublai Khan was able to overthrow** the Chinese emperor and install a new dynasty, the Yuan dynasty, in the 1270s.

780. **The most devastating defeats the Mongols suffered were their invasions of Japan** in 1274 and 1281.

781. **The Mongols conquered medieval Russia, emerging as the new rulers of the Russian people** for the next few centuries.

782. **The Mongols significantly weakened many Muslim empires in the Middle East** by **defeating the Ayyubid Sultanate** and taking the city of Baghdad from the last **Abbasid caliph** in 1258.

783. **The siege of Baghdad was one of the most significant Mongol victories.** The city was ruthlessly sacked by the Mongols, and the Abbasid dynasty was put to an end.

784. **Another decisive victory would be achieved in modern-day Turkey against the Sultanate of Rum at Kose Dag in 1243.** This victory would mark the beginning of the decline of Seljuk Turkish rule in Anatolia.

785. **The Egyptian Mamluks would put a stop to Mongol invasions in the Islamic world,** defeating them in the 13th century and signing a peace treaty at Aleppo.

786. **The Mongol conquest brought about complete devastation in many places,** but Mongol dominance also ushered in a period of economic and cultural exchange.

787. **The Mongols were responsible for improved trade routes between eastern Asia and western Europe** through central Asian cities like Bukhara, Samarkand, Herat, and Merv, which they all controlled.

788. **Under Mongol rule, some areas experienced a period of peace, such as present-day Kazakhstan,** where nomadic tribes enjoyed relative stability due to the lack of resistance from local rulers.

789. **The Mongols were known to tolerate different religions and cultures in the territories they conquered,** allowing people to practice their faith without discrimination or persecution.

790. **The Mongols taxed conquered peoples to assert their political dominance over them.**

791. **During the Mongol conquests of the Middle East and the Levant, the Mongols** were exposed to Islam. Some Mongols willingly converted.

792. **The Mongols had a very effective communication system called Yam,** which allowed messages to be sent across vast distances within a short timeframe, with horse riders using relay stations.

793. **The invasions were responsible for spreading diseases across Eurasia,** such as the bubonic plague, during their campaigns in the 1340s.

794. **Genghis Khan is widely regarded as one of history's greatest and most influential leaders.**

795. **During these invasions, many cities across Eurasia saw an influx in population due to refugees seeking** safety from destruction caused by invading armies.

796. **The Mongol invasions also saw an increased use of gunpowder weapons,** such as cannons, which helped them immensely when attacking fortified cities or castles.

797. **At times, the Mongols destroyed books and manuscripts from libraries.** This was likely done to show dominance and prevent the spread of rebellious ideas.

798. **Mongolian culture was heavily influenced by the people they conquered during their campaigns,** with cultures being blended together to form a unique Mongol identity.

799. **One famous figure associated with the Mongol era is Marco Polo,** who is said to have traveled through much of Asia while serving in Kublai Khan's court in what's now known as modern-day Beijing, China.

800. In general, **the Mongol invasions had far-reaching implications throughout Eurasia that impacted military tactics** and cultural exchange between different nations for centuries.

The Rise of the Ottoman Empire
(13th-15th centuries)

A look at the rise of the Ottoman Empire is in order to understand how the Ottomans grew strong enough to take the capital of Constantinople in 1456. These thirty facts will unpack how the Ottoman Empire was ruled and the influential figures who helped the empire gain power.

801. **The Ottoman Empire was a Turkish empire that controlled much of Anatolia, western Asia,** the Balkans, and North Africa at its peak.

802. **The empire had its origins in Anatolia at the end of the 13th century** and reached the height of its power in the 16th century.

803. **The name "Ottoman" comes from Osman,** the founder of the Ottoman dynasty in Anatolia.

804. **Osman was the leader of one of the Turkish beyliks—small political Muslim states—**that increasingly appeared in Anatolia after the decline of **the Sultanate of Rum** in the 13th century.

805. **These beyliks were concentrated in different provinces of Asia Minor** but shared much of the same culture and socioeconomic makeup. However, they were still largely politically unstable and, therefore, inferior to neighboring states in the region.

806. **The Anatolian beyliks had complex relations with each other and strove for dominance in the region, though they were all followers of Islam.**

807. **While not a lot is known about Osman, we do know he was the leader of a beylik located in the northwestern part of Asia Minor** in the historical Byzantine province of Bithynia.

808. **During Osman's rule in the late 13th century, he slowly expanded his control in the area, overcoming resistance from the Byzantine Empire,** which had already entered its period of decline, and from neighboring beyliks.

809. **The crucial turning point would come in 1326 when the Ottomans**, under the leadership of Osman's son, Orhan, managed to capture the city of Bursa in Anatolia from the Byzantines. They made the city their capital.

810. **At that time, Byzantine holdings were concentrated in an area around Constantinople,** so the Ottomans continued to wage their war against them and other nations of the Balkans, like the Bulgars and the Serbs.

811. **The Ottoman warriors considered themselves the ghazi,** warriors who fought in the name of Muhammad to spread Islam to non-Muslim people.

812. **The Ottomans had a somewhat clearly defined goal and objective** (spread their religion). **The materialization of this goal was the prized city of Constantinople,** which was not only one of the richest places in the world at that point but also a major center of Christianity.

813. **Throughout the first half of the 14th century, the Ottomans emerged victorious from most of their campaigns in the west, capturing the Greek city of Thessaloniki** from the Republic of Venice in 1387 and **defeating the Serbians at the Battle of Kosovo** in 1389.

814. **These victories consolidated Ottoman possessions in the Balkans** even more,

prompting a response from other European Christian nations. These nations decided to form a coalition and confront the Ottomans a few years later.

815. In September 1396, **the Ottoman forces fought a decisive battle against a united European army** that consisted of contingents from Hungary, Croatia, France, Bulgaria, Genoa, Venice, and the Byzantine Empire. The allied army was headed by **King Sigismund of Hungary and Croatia.**

816. **These nations believed that potential Muslim expansion into eastern Europe was against their collective interests** and assembled a force of about twenty thousand to face the Ottomans at Nicopolis. This confrontation is sometimes referred to as the final large-scale Crusade of the Middle Ages.

817. **Despite the efforts of the Crusaders, the Ottoman forces, under Sultan Bayezid I,** were able to decisively defeat them at Nicopolis, establishing a permanent Ottoman presence in the region.

818. **The Ottomans were temporarily stopped at the beginning of the 15th century** when Anatolia was invaded and ransacked by the Timurids under their leader, Tamerlane. **The Ottomans were defeated at the Battle of Ankara** in 1402, and Sultan Bayezid was captured.

819. **This defeat was followed by about a decade of instability in the Ottoman state.** The Ottomans lost their newly gained territories in the Balkans and suffered a civil war, which eventually ended with the emergence of **Mehmed I as the new sultan.**

820. After having regained control, **the Ottomans turned their attention to the Byzantine capital, with Sultan Mehmed II besieging Constantinople in 1453 with an army of about 100,000.**

821. **By then, the Byzantine Empire had been reduced to essentially only the city of Constantinople.** While the city was well fortified, it only had about ten thousand men to defend it.

822. **The Ottomans were able to break through the Byzantine defenses** after a fifty-three-day siege, during which they maintained a full naval and land blockade of the city and bombarded its walls with artillery.

823. **The siege of Constantinople was one of the first major battles where the Ottomans** were able to demonstrate the devastating power of gunpowder weapons, which were still a relative novelty at that time.

824. **The fall of Constantinople in May 1453 marked the end of the Byzantine Empire** and is also one of the dates considered to be the end of **the Late Middle Ages.**

825. **Mehmed II, known as Mehmed the Conqueror,** was quite tolerant of **the Orthodox** population in the city and maintained the autonomy of **the Christian Church.**

826. **Mehmed II is regarded as one of the most successful sultans of the Ottoman Empire,** as he introduced a range of military and sociopolitical reforms that strengthened the state.

827. **After the conquest of Constantinople, Mehmed renamed the city Istanbul.**

828. **Sultan Mehmed II ordered the construction of the famous Topkapi Palace,** a magnificent complex that would house the center of Ottoman administration for many centuries after its completion.

829. **The Ottoman Empire continued its expansion in the coming decades, reaching the height of its dominance under the reign of Sultan Suleiman the Magnificent in the 16th century.**

830. **Ottoman society, much like other Muslim societies in the Middle Ages,** was organized in accordance with the Islamic Sharia law, something that reached into all aspects of everyday life.

The Hanseatic League
(13th–17th centuries)

This chapter will explore the fascinating history of the Hanseatic League and its contribution to Europe's culture, economy, and politics. Let's dive into some interesting facts about why it was created and who was part of it.

831. **The Hanseatic League was an economic and defensive alliance of merchant guilds, cities, and their allies in northern Europe.**

832. **Its members included cities on major trade routes throughout northern Europe,** including **Bruges** (Belgium), **Hamburg** (Germany), **Visby** (Sweden), and **Gdansk** (Poland).

833. **Hanseatic ships sailed between these ports, carrying grain, herring oil, fish products** like caviar or salted codfish, timber for shipbuilding, flax and linen cloth, and much else.

834. **At its peak, it had around 170 member towns spread over seven countries,** from Estonia in the east to the Netherlands in the west.

835. **The league was not based on a complex set of multinational charters like international organizations are today.** Instead, the members of the Hanseatic League relied on each other's informal relations to foster trade and development.

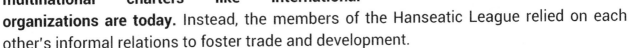
836. **Hanse is a German word that means "band" or "group." During the Middle Ages, its meaning changed to refer to a society of merchants.**

837. **The Hanseatic League was an early example of a free trade agreement,** with members protecting each other's interests in foreign markets.

838. **It played a major role in developing international finance and provided banking services to its member cities.**

839. **As the league spread across Europe, it gained political influence,** becoming one of the most influential organizations in medieval times.

840. **The city of Lübeck, though relatively small today,** was a central point in **the Hanseatic League** due to its convenient location.

841. **To accelerate Lübeck's status as a trading center,** it granted special privileges **to Scandinavian and Russian traders.**

842. **Lübeck also gained special favors with the papacy and the Catholic world,** as it was the main port used by **the Crusaders during the Northern Crusades,** which were directed against the pagan populations of **the Baltic and Scandinavia.**

843. In 1226, **Lübeck became a free imperial city by a charter granted to it by Holy Roman Emperor Frederick II.**

844. **Being a free imperial city meant Lübeck had special privileges,** like an increased degree of political autonomy and a place in the Holy Roman Empire's imperial diet.

845. **Hamburg, Bremen, Wismar, and many other cities would also receive these benefits as the importance of the Hanseatic League began to increase.**

846. **For a time, these cities even shared a common currency – the Hohlplenning – which was originally minted in Lübeck** and was later adopted by Hamburg and Wismar to make transactions easier.

847. **The Hanseatic League began declining by the end of the 16th century due to external factors,** such as increased competition from Dutch and English merchants.

848. **Merchants began to increasingly rely on Atlantic Ocean routes rather than the Baltic Sea** routes favored by many Hansa members.

849. **In the 17th century, Sweden conquered much of the territory previously controlled by Denmark-Norway,** forcing several Hansa towns to become part of the Swedish Empire.

850. **The Hanseatic League was never formally dissolved,** but it lost any real power it had by 1669.

851. **The Hanseatic League was an early example of regional organization and cooperation,** paving the way for modern European Union institutions, such as the Council of Europe or the Eurozone.

852. **Members were bound by a legal framework allowing them to act together on specific issues,** thus making it one of the earliest known organizations with federal characteristics.

853. **Some of the trading activities that took place in port cities centuries ago have left behind some amazing buildings.** These warehouses, called kontors, can still be seen today and are popular tourist attractions.

854. **In addition to its economic importance, the Hanseatic League also had cultural influence.** It was responsible for the spread of the German language and culture to Nordic countries.

855. **The Hanseatic League played an essential role in promoting education, science, and literature** among members by providing support for universities and libraries.

856. **Being part of the league enabled merchants to avoid paying taxes that others had to pay.**

857. **Hanseatic merchants didn't have to follow the same trade regulations** as other merchants. They also didn't have the same travel restrictions.

858. **The Hansa is credited with standardizing weights and measuring currency exchange rates,** allowing for more efficient commerce.

859. **There was an extensive network of alliances between member cities and non-member ones,** allowing them to coordinate actions when threatened by foreign powers.

860. **Despite all its obstacles during its long history, the Hanseatic League was one of the most successful medieval organizations,** leaving an indelible mark on Europe's culture and economic politics.

Poland and Hungary in the Middle Ages

So many regions, so little time. Let's take a look at a few regions that are not often talked about when it comes to the Middle Ages. These thirty facts will hopefully pique your interest in learning more about Poland's and Hungary's histories!

861. **At the time of the collapse of the Western Roman Empire,** not much was known about the area east of Germania in modern-day eastern Europe.

862. **However, this region would emerge to be one of the most diverse during the Middle Ages,** with many different interesting and powerful kingdoms being established.

863. **Two powerful Christian kingdoms would eventually start to take shape in these areas: Poland and Hungary.**

864. **The history of what would eventually become the Kingdom of Poland** began with the establishment of **the state of Polanie** under **the rule of Mieszko I,** who is often considered the first ruler of Poland (c. 960–992).

865. **Mieszko I's conversion to Catholicism in 966 marked the Christianization of Poland.** His baptism is closely linked with the creation of the Polish state.

866. **Although the Great Schism had not yet happened, missionaries from the Greek and the Latin Church journeyed out to lands not yet converted to Christianity** to spread their own form of the religion.

867. **Gniezno in western Poland was the first capital of the early Polish state.**

868. **The Battle of Cedynia in 972 is considered one of the earliest recorded battles in Polish history and resulted in a victory over the Germans,** further securing Poland's western borders.

869. **The reign of Bolesław I the Brave** (r. 1025), **the son of Mieszko, saw the establishment of the Kingdom of Poland**, with its capital in **Kraków. Bolesław** was crowned the first king of Poland.

870. **Bolesław is considered one of the most accomplished Polish rulers of all time.** During his reign as the duke of Poland, he battled extensively with **the Holy Roman Empire** and even managed to briefly conquer Kiev in 1018.

871. **In the 12th and 13th centuries, a period of fragmentation took place,** with Poland being divided into multiple smaller duchies and principalities.

872. **The Mongol invasions of the 13th century led to the destruction of many Polish cities and settlements.** The Polish were defeated by the Mongols at the Battle of Legnica in 1241, but the Mongols had to withdraw to address a succession dispute.

873. **Bolesław V the Chaste** (r. 1243–1279) **reestablished Polish unity** and centralized power during the 13th century.

874. **Around the same time, the Teutonic Knights established themselves in Prussia and Pomerania.** They often came into conflict with Poland.

875. **Over time, the Teutonic Knights would grow their possessions, emerging as one of the most stalwart defenders of Christianity** in the region and participating in the important political developments in the Baltic region.

876. **Poland was a feudal society, but its social organization was heavily dependent on the nobility.** Over time, the nobles began to gain more and more power, leading to the eventual establishment of the so-called **"Golden Liberty."**

877. **The Golden Liberty was a system in late medieval Poland that granted all nobles,** despite their actual social standing, wealth, or ethnicity, a multitude of legal rights and privileges while also granting them control of the state's legislature.

878. In 1333, **King Casimir III the Great issued the Statute of Kalisz,** which granted rights and protections to Poland's Jewish population, making Poland one of the more tolerant countries for Jews in medieval Europe.

879. **In 1386, the Kingdom of Poland and the Grand Duchy of Lithuania** entered into a personal union with the marriage of **Queen Jadwiga of Poland and Grand Duke Jogaila of Lithuania.** This union was called **the Union of Krewo.**

880. **Lithuanian Grand Duke Jogaila, who took the name Władysław II Jagiełło** upon converting to Christianity, became **the king of Poland.**

881. **The kings of Poland-Lithuania would eventually be elected by the nobles,** much like the practice that was present in **the Holy Roman Empire.**

882. **The Kingdom of Hungary emerged in the late 9th century when Árpád,** the leader of the Hungarian tribes, founded **the Principality of Hungary.**

883. **Stephen I, also known as Saint Stephen, was crowned as the first Christian king of Hungary in 1000.** His reign marked the official conversion of Hungary to Christianity.

884. **The Hungarian monarchy adopted Christianity from the Roman Catholic Church** and became a significant Catholic kingdom in central Europe.

885. **The Árpád dynasty ruled Hungary for several centuries,** establishing a stable and powerful kingdom.

886. **The Golden Bull of 1222 was a royal charter that granted significant rights and privileges to the Hungarian nobility,** influencing the development of Hungary's political system.

887. **The Battle of Mohi in 1241 was a disastrous defeat for Hungary.** The Mongols' victory led to widespread destruction and upheaval.

888. **Béla IV** (r. 1235–1270) **is known for rebuilding the country after the Mongol invasions** and for introducing stone castles and fortifications.

889. **The era of dominance for these two kingdoms falls a bit outside of the conventional date of the Middle Ages,** as both began to significantly increase their domains from the 16th century onward.

890. **The geographical locations of the kingdoms of Poland and Hungary made them crossroads for a multitude of cultures and peoples,** leading to unique social circumstances that would continue to develop after the Renaissance.

The Hundred Years' War
(1337–1453)

The Hundred Years' War was a 116-year-long conflict between England and France that had a significant impact on European history. Let's explore how devastating this battle was and why it was even fought in the first place.

891. **The Hundred Years' War was a conflict fought primarily between the Kingdom of England and the Kingdom of France.** It lasted from 1337 to 1453.

892. **The war was longer than one hundred years, but the fighting wasn't constant.** There were times when there was no fighting. According to some historians, the war should be called the **Eight-one Years' War!**

893. **King Charles IV, of the French house of Capet,** had no heirs and no brothers, and the conflict began in 1337 with his death, as the closest male relative of his was his nephew – **Edward III of England.**

894. The situation escalated when **Edward III of England claimed sovereignty over the French throne in 1337** following his mother Isabella's claim (Charles' sister) to it as heir through her father, **Philip IV of France.**

895. **Edward III proclaimed himself king of France, although this claim was never officially recognized by the French nobility,** who naturally wanted a Frenchman as king. However, it led to considerable diplomatic tension between **England and France** over succession rights.

896. In addition to dynastic claims, other causes for **the breakout of the war include a long-standing rivalry between the English and French kingdoms and territorial disputes.**

897. **The war was fought on several fronts, including Aquitaine in the southwest, Brittany in the north, and Flanders in the east.**

898. The war saw many battles fought over castles, including **Harfleur (1415)**, **Agincourt (1415)** and **Crecy (1346)**.

899. **The English were initially successful, winning battles at Crécy and Poitiers,** but they steadily lost ground in the 1400s.

900. **In 1348, the bubonic plague claimed an estimated twenty-five million lives in Europe.** This was known as the Black Death or Great Pestilence, and it severely impacted both sides, leading to a pause in the fighting.

901. **In 1356, Edward, Prince of Wales** (known as the Black Prince) won **the Battle of Poitiers,** where he captured **King John II of France,** who was later released after **the Treaty of Brétigny** was signed.

902. In 1360, **Edward III signed the Treaty of Brétigny, which ended his claim to the throne but ceded large parts of western France** (including Aquitaine) to England. This truce only lasted for nine years before Charles V of France re-declared war in 1369.

903. **King John II returned to France, but his son, Louis of Anjou,** was sent to England while John came up with the ransom payment. When Louis escaped confinement, John II returned to England rather than face dishonor.

904. **The Battle of Agincourt, fought in October 1415,** was a decisive victory for the English and one of the most famous battles fought during **the Hundred Years' War.** This battle was immortalized by **Shakespeare in his play Henry V.**

905. **The English won significant victories at sea, such as Sluys (1340)** and **La Rochelle (1372),** but many ships were lost to French privateers operating out of harbors like **Harfleur and Dieppe.**

906. **English forces also laid siege to major cities, such as Rouen,** which held out for nearly six months before surrendering in 1419 due to famine and disease.

907. Henry VI became king of England in 1429 and was king of France in 1431. His uncle, Charles, contested his claim to the French throne.

908. Charles's father had previously ruled France. However, **Charles was known as the Dauphin** until he was crowned.

909. Jeanne d'Arc, also known as Joan of Arc, was born into a poor family in the small village of Domrémy around 1412. She claimed to have visions from God that told her she was destined to help France win its freedom from the English.

910. In May 1429, she led French forces against an English army occupying Orléans and won a victory for the Dauphin of France.

911. The Dauphin was crowned king at Rheims Cathedral in July 1429. He became King Charles VII.

912. Joan would later be captured by the English and sentenced to burn at the stake. She is remembered as the woman who rallied the French when they were at one of their lowest points in the war.

913. The English were ultimately defeated by French forces under Charles VII at the Battle of Castillon (1453), leading to the end of **the Hundred Years' War.**

914. The war provided a backdrop for some of history's most significant figures, such as **Edward III, Henry V, Joan of Arc, Richard II, and John Talbot, who all left their mark on this period in time.**

915. During the Hundred Years' War, taxation increased drastically in England, with levies being imposed on wool exports and other imports; this caused significant unrest among people, making the toll of the war heavier on the ordinary population the longer the war went on.

916. In 1381, the Peasants' Revolt broke out across England, resulting in large-scale destruction and murder. The revolt is thought to have been caused by the high taxes imposed on the English people during the war.

917. England's economy suffered greatly during the Hundred Years' War due to lost battles and increased taxation. Many people left the country in search of better opportunities elsewhere.

918. The Hundred Years' War had disastrous effects on France. Tens of thousands died in battles, and many more died due to illness or starvation. The Black Death had a disastrous impact on the French population during the war.

919. English longbowmen were a key military unit during the Hundred Years' War due to their superior range over traditional crossbows. They played an essential role in victories, like at Crécy.

920. The war saw the increased use of mercenaries on both sides, **including Swiss pikemen and Italian crossbowmen;** wealthy nobles or merchants often paid for their services, even employing some in their private regiments.

921. One significant development was the heavy use of artillery, which allowed armies to breach castle walls more easily than before. This changed siege warfare significantly but also had drawbacks when used in field battles due to slow reload times.

922. England retained control over certain parts of France known as the Pale of Calais until 1558, when it finally fell into French hands after a long siege.

923. The Hundred Years' War is often seen as the first "modern" war due to its lengthy duration, complex political alliances, and new technologies used on both sides, including gunpowder in cannons and handguns, which were still relatively rare at that time.

924. France came out of the war as the victor. The war led to a greater sense of French national identity and the increased centralization of government. England lost its claims to the French throne and the disputed lands.

925. The Hundred Years' War was a significant event in the history of medieval Europe. It resulted in new advances in technology, strategy, tactics, and weaponry.

The Black Death
(1347–1351)

The Black Death was the most devastating pandemic in recorded human history, claiming the lives of millions of people across Eurasia. Discover how the Black Death got its name and how people in medieval times explained the cause of the disease with these interesting facts.

926. **The Black Death was one of the most devastating pandemics in human history,** killing an estimated twenty-five to two hundred million people across Eurasia.

927. **The Black Death was primarily a bubonic plague pandemic, but many scholars believe people suffered from septicemic and pneumonic plague as well.**

928. **The name "Black Death" comes from the dark patches on victims' skin due to blood circulation** problems caused by the disease.

929. **Symptoms included fever, headache, vomiting,** coughing up blood, and extreme fatigue.

930. **During the Black Death, the disease often led to death within three to five days after infection.**

931. **During its peak in Europe (1347–1351), it killed** approximately 30 percent of Europe's population.

932. **In some areas, mortality rates were even higher, with 60 to 90 percent of** populations being wiped out.

933. **In addition to people, animals, including pigs, cows, sheep, and chickens, also perished due to this epidemic.**

934. **The Black Death spread in four waves,** starting in central Asia and spreading to Europe via the Silk Road and maritime routes.

935. **It reached the largest cities of the Italian peninsula by 1348,** England by 1349, and had affected all of Europe by 1350.

936. It was believed that rats were one of the leading carriers of the plague, although research suggests other animals, such as gerbils, may have been responsible for its spread.

937. The Black Death was actually caused by a flea called Yersinia pestis. The fleas would attach themselves to rodents, which would then go on to infect humans.

938. Recent studies are beginning to uncover the idea that human fleas and lice were more responsible for the spread than fleas on rodents.

939. People back then had many theories about what caused the plague, including bad air (the miasma theory), divine punishment, or even a comet crashing into Earth's atmosphere.

940. People tried various remedies, from burning incense to wearing garlic around their necks, to prevent infection, but nothing seemed to work.

941. People believed they could prevent infection by drinking vinegar or covering themselves with herbs such as lavender.

942. In some cities, like Venice, laws dealt with how people handled dead bodies. They had to be buried immediately in mass graves without any ceremonies.

943. To stop the disease from spreading, trade routes between countries were closed off, completely preventing supplies from coming in or out, which led to food shortages and rising prices.

944. As a result of the Black Death, wages rose significantly due to a shortage of workers to do jobs.

945. The pope called for prayers throughout Europe, but this did little to stop the spread of the plague.

946. Some people turned away from God, believing he had abandoned them, which led to the church losing power.

947. **An interesting movement that became prominent during the Black Death was flagellantism,** a radical Christian practice whose followers aimed to humble themselves by whipping their skin with different instruments.

948. **Flagellants believed the pandemic was God's punishment to humanity,** and they dramatically increased their activities, blaming themselves and even hosting public rituals.

949. **Some cities like Venice set quarantine laws,** meaning anyone entering or leaving had to be separated to prevent the spread of infection.

950. **Heavily urbanized areas, like big cities, were the most affected**, especially since there was no real regulation of sanitation.

951. **At times, soldiers would use victims of the plague as biological weapons.** Armies would hurl dead bodies that had been infected with the plague with catapults over to enemy lines, hoping to spread the disease in their ranks.

952. **Many of the survivors were left deeply traumatized.** Some even developed psychological problems, such as paranoia and depression.

953. **After its initial spread, outbreaks occurred for another four hundred years across Europe,** sometimes lasting for months at a time.

954. **In some places, people blamed Jews for causing the plague,** leading to increased antisemitism and violence against Jewish communities.

955. **It is believed that a combination of natural causes and human intervention helped bring about the end to the Black Death,** such as improved sanitation practices and increased public health measures.

The Decline of Feudalism
(14th–16th centuries)

This chapter will explore the decline of feudalism in Europe, which began in the 14th century and gradually ended in the 16th century. We'll look at some interesting facts about what led people to think about feudalism in a different way than before.

956. **One of the main reasons for feudalism's decline was the rise in centralized monarchies,** which decreased the importance of lesser regional lords.

957. **Another important factor contributing to its decline was technological advancements,** such as gunpowder, crossbows, and longbows, which made cavalry-based warfare obsolete, leading to an increase in infantry forces that further weakened **the feudal structure's reliance on knights.**

958. **Trade also played an essential role since it enabled people to access goods that weren't available locally before,** which led to an improvement in living standards within towns and cities and reduced a person's dependence upon their manor.

959. **During this period, people began to move away from rural areas toward cities in search of better job opportunities.**

960. **Changes in religious beliefs caused by the Reformation also affected loyalty to feudal lords, decreasing their influence.**

961. **People who belonged to a different faith than the majority population had another way of seeking guidance,** which caused them to be less devoted to their lord.

962. **This period saw an increase in literacy and education with the advent of the printing press in the 16th century,** which further weakened the feudal system since people had better access to new ideas or information previously censored by religious and government authorities.

963. The Black Death is credited with hastening feudalism's decline since it wiped out a big portion of the population, leading to labor shortages and weakening feudalism's reliance upon serfdom.

964. The competition from other economic systems, like mercantilism, made feudalism less popular. Mercantilism is an economic belief that one should focus more on maximizing profits through trade rather than relying upon subsistence-level production.

965. Feudal laws were gradually replaced by law codes, which were seen as more modern than traditional methods used in earlier centuries.

966. This period saw the emergence of nation-states. Instead of disparate regions or kingdoms ruled by one monarch, a unified nation oversaw the people.

967. Trade guilds became more powerful during this period and could influence politics and the economy by controlling production and pricing, which further weakened the serfs' reliance upon lords for protection or sustenance.

968. The decline of feudalism meant the weakening of serfdom. Peasants had greater freedom over their lives since they were no longer bound by their obligations toward lordly families who previously held sway over them due to ownership rights.

969. The end of feudalism ushered in an era where money was king as opposed to before, when land, titles, and ranks played a much more significant role.

970. Feudalism's demise opened doors for new social classes, like middle-class merchants who could exploit opportunities thanks to feudalism's collapse while also avoiding the hurdles the ruling upper echelons could pose.

The Crisis of the Late Middle Ages
(13th–14th centuries)

There is no definitive end to the Middle Ages, although most historians use the year 1453 (the year Constantinople fell to the Ottoman Empire) as a convenient stopping point. This section will take a look at some of the major problems that occurred at the end of the Middle Ages.

971. **The Crisis of the Middle Ages refers to a period of profound upheaval and transformation that affected Europe during the late 13th and early 14th centuries.**

972. **This crisis encompassed a range of interconnected factors,** including social and environmental challenges like overpopulation, climate change, and changes in agricultural practices.

973. **Europe experienced a population boom during the High Middle Ages,** leading to increased demand for resources.

974. **Rapid urbanization in the 12th and 13th centuries was a significant part of the High Middle Ages,** with many European towns and cities growing in size and importance.

975. **The growth of towns and cities led to increased commerce, trade, and cultural exchange.**

976. **Trade routes like the Silk Road facilitated the exchange of goods, ideas, and technologies between Europe and the East.**

977. **The rise of a money-based economy and the development of banking systems** contributed to the economic prosperity of many urban centers.

978. **However, a high level of urbanization was not supported since there was not an increase in the number of available jobs in the cities.**

979. For the most part, **the social organization of Europe** was largely agrarian and based in rural areas.

980. **The cities suffered from overpopulation,** with many people being reduced to poverty.

981. **In major cities, slums were created,** and sanitation was very poor.

982. **This coincided with the spread of the Black Death,** which decimated at least a third of Europe's population by the mid-14th century.

983. **Because of the circumstances created in the major urban centers,** the plague spread quickly. It is believed Venice and Florence lost up to two-thirds of their population.

984. **People were also affected by wars, such as the Hundred Years' War,** which began in 1337. Conflicts like this spread the Black Death as well, leading to more deaths.

985. **Deforestation and the overuse of land for agriculture had adverse environmental effects,** including soil degradation and the loss of arable land.

986. **Farmers had used the ancient practice of growing their crops over and over again on the same land,** something that decreased the quality of the land and the number of yields each year.

987. **People in Europe suffered from widespread food shortages caused by crop failure and low yields.**

988. **The 14th century saw the beginning of what's known as the Little Ice Age,** a period of regional cooling that saw a general decrease in temperatures. This period lasted until the 19th century.

989. **The population of Europe was not prepared for such a dramatic climate change,** which also exacerbated the food shortage that had already existed because of the plague and soil degradation.

990. **The crisis had far-reaching effects on European society,** eventually contributing to the transition from the Middle Ages to the Early Modern period.

991. Many states experienced domestic instability. The fragmentation of feudal states contributed to the crisis.

992. Europe's economic crisis led to inflation and dealt a blow to the medieval manorial system.

993. The Crisis of the Late Middle Ages weakened the Catholic Church's authority, as it struggled to provide spiritual guidance and deal with the suffering caused by **the Black Death.**

994. Many minority groups that were deemed heretical were persecuted. They were often used as scapegoats for the hardships people were experiencing.

995. Many artistic and literary works from this period, like the writings by Petrarch and Boccaccio, reflected a somber mood and themes of mortality.

996. Europe eventually began to recover from the crisis in the late 14th and early 15th centuries.

997. Advances in trade and navigation, like the voyages of discovery and the expansion of maritime routes, opened up new economic opportunities.

998. Developments in farming techniques, like crop rotation, introduced well-needed changes to agricultural practice.

999. The Renaissance, a cultural and intellectual movement, emerged during the late 14th and 15th centuries. It brought a renewed interest in classical learning and art and inspired scientific and technological developments.

1000. The Crisis of the Middle Ages represents a pivotal moment in European history, as it reshaped the continent in profound ways.

Conclusion

The medieval times were an era of awe-inspiring complexity, filled with tales of heroism and struggle. Through this book, we have explored the core facts that shaped this period in history, **from the rise of Christianity to Charlemagne's reign, from feudalism to Viking expansion, and from the Crusades to the Hundred Years' War.** We also uncovered fascinating facts about **Muslim expansion, the papacy, and the rise of universities.** We learned the impact of **the Mongol invasions** and **the Hanseatic League** while appreciating **Gothic architecture.**

The Middle Ages was a time of tremendous change, and these fun facts only skimmed the surface of what you can learn about this period. **We highly encourage you to pinpoint the topics** that interest you the most and explore them further.

Thanks for joining us on this journey!

If you enjoyed this book, a review on Amazon would be greatly appreciated because it would mean a lot to hear from you.

To leave a review:

1. Open your camera app.
2. Point your mobile device at the QR code.
3. The review page will appear in your web browser.

Thanks for your support!

Check out another book in the series

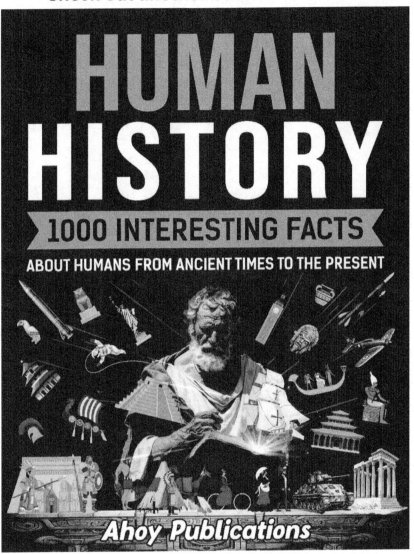

Welcome Aboard, Check Out This Limited-Time Free Bonus!

Ahoy, reader! Welcome to the Ahoy Publications family, and thanks for snagging a copy of this book! Since you've chosen to join us on this journey, we'd like to offer you something special.

Check out the link below for a FREE e-book filled with delightful facts about American History.

But that's not all - you'll also have access to our exclusive email list with even more free e-books and insider knowledge. Well, what are ye waiting for? Click the link below to join and set sail toward exciting adventures in American History.

Access your bonus here: <u>https://ahoypublications.com/</u>

<u>Or, Scan the QR code!</u>

Sources and Additional References

Grant, Robert M. A Short History of the Interpretation of the Bible: The Ancient Period. Westminster John Knox Press, 2007.

Bradshaw, Paul F., ed. Early Christian World. Taylor & Francis Group LLC, 2010.

De Vries, Simon. An Introduction to Medieval Europe 300-1500. Cambridge University Press, 2012.

Freedman, Paul H., ed. The Oxford Encyclopedia of the Middle Ages: Volume 4 - Christianity in Western Europe and Expansion Beyond 600–1500 A.D. Oxford University Press, 2010.

Cormack, Margaret. The Barbarian Invasions of Europe and the Migration Period: From Caesar to Attila the Hun. Pen & Sword History, 2019.

Jones, Lesley. Barbarians: An Exploration of the Savage World. National Geographic Society, 2017.

Kern-Stähler, Annette and Jörg Rogge (ed.). The Barbarian Invasions: History and Legacy of the Migrations that Shaped Medieval Europe. ABC-CLIO, 2019.

Scarre, Chris. The Penguin Historical Atlas of Ancient Rome. New York: Penguin Books, 1995.

Towne, David A., et al. Europe in the Middle Ages: An Encyclopedia for Students. New York: Routledge Taylor & Francis Group, 2017.

Theissen, Gary. Charlemagne: Empire and Society. Manchester University Press, 2005.

Jones, Jonathan and David Nicolle. Charlemagne: A Military Biography of the Great Emperor Who United Europe in the Early Middle Ages. Osprey Publishing Ltd., 2020.

Jones, Johnathan and Roberta Miller. A History of Feudalism: Tenure and Service in Medieval Europe 900-1400 CE. Routledge Press, 2019.

Curran Jr., William J. The Age of Chivalry: Life in the Middle Ages 1066 - 1485 AD. Atlantic Publishing Co., 2018.

Turner, Ralph V. The Magna Carta: A Very Short Introduction. Oxford University Press, 2014.

James, David. Viking Expansion: A Historical Overview. Edinburgh University Press, 2018.

Runciman, Steven. A History of the Crusades: Volume II. Cambridge University Press, 1955.

Tyerman, Christopher. The Oxford Illustrated History of the Crusades. Oxford University Press 2006.

Williams, Rowan A. The Great Schism: A History of the Papal Divide Between East and West. Princeton UP, 2016.

Deaux, George. The Black Death 1347–1352: The Complete History. Thomas Dunne Books, 2004.

Webster, T. R., and Christine Carpenter. The Hundred Years' War: A People's History. Yale University Press, 2009.

Smith, Sean. The Black Death: An Epic History of Plague and Pestilence. Simon & Schuster, 2008.

Yousuf, Imran. The Islamic Empires: A Historical Encyclopedia. ABC-CLIO, 2018.

Duffy, Eamon. Saints & Sinners: A History of the Popes. Yale University Press, 2001.

Crousset, F. (1996). The Mongol Empire: Genghis Khan, His Heirs and the Founding of Modern China. New York: St Martin's Press.

Brubaker, Patrick. Warfare and Society in the Mongol World. Routledge, 2017.

Ryan, Shannon. The Hanseatic League: A Maritime History of the Middle Ages. McFarland & Company Inc., 2013.

Bull, Marcus. The Hanseatic League: A History. Oxford University Press, 2018.

Herzog, Don. The Spanish Inquisition: A Historical Revision. Yale University Press, 1998.

McNeill, William H. The Great Famine: Northern Europe in the Early Fourteenth Century. University of Chicago Press, 2020.

Printed in Great Britain
by Amazon

51183626R00071